# Kiwiana Cupcakes, Cake Pops *and* Whoopie Pies

**HarperCollins*Publishers***

First published in 2013
by HarperCollins*Publishers (New Zealand) Limited*
PO Box 1, Shortland Street, Auckland 1140

Text copyright © Kirsten Day 2013
Photography copyright © Charlie Smith 2013

Kirsten Day and Charlie Smith assert the moral right to be identified as the author and photographer of this work.
All rights reserved. No part of this publication may be reproduced, stored in a retrieval system or transmitted in any form or by any means, electronic, mechanical, photocopying, recording or otherwise, without the prior written permission of the publishers.

**HarperCollins*Publishers***
Printed in China by RR Donnelly on 128gsm Huaxia Sun Matte Art
Level 13, 201 Elizabeth Street, Sydney, NSW 2000, Australia
A 53, Sector 57, Noida, UP, India
77–85 Fulham Palace Road, London W6 8JB, United Kingdom
2 Bloor Street East, 20th floor, Toronto, Ontario M4W 1A8, Canada
195 Broadway, New York, NY 10007, USA

National Library of New Zealand Cataloguing-in-Publication Data
Day, Kirsten.
Kiwiana cupcakes / Kirsten Day.
Includes index.
ISBN 978-1-77554-025-0
1. Cupcakes. 2. Baking. II. Title.
641.8653—dc 23

ISBN: 978 1 77554 025 0

Cover and internal design by Carolyn Lewis
Publisher: Bill Honeybone

Printed by RR Donnelley, China

02 03 04   14

# Kiwiana Cupcakes, Cake Pops and Whoopie Pies

## Kirsten Day

♥

*Photography by* Charlie Smith

# Contents

Introduction  7

Hints and Tips  9

Tools and Equipment  20

Kiwiana Cupcakes  27

Cupcake Recipes  90

Kiwiana Cake Pops  100

Cake Pop Cake Recipes  114

Whoopie Pies  118

Fillings for Whoopie Pies  130

Icings  132

Conversion Tables  140

Acknowledgements  141

Index  142

# Introduction

If Kiwiana defines what it is to be a New Zealander, to me it has meant growing up in the great outdoors with the freedom to grow and explore! When I was asked to put together some Kiwiana-themed cupcakes for this book I was overwhelmed with excitement and ideas. Where to start? I grew up in semi-rural New Zealand so items of Kiwiana were never far away. My inspiration for many of the cupcakes in this book was childhood memories of holidays and experiences growing up in our slice of paradise.

As life gets busier I have to remind myself to always take the time to 'smell the roses'. When driving from Auckland down the island to Palmerston North to visit my family I get the chance to do that, and I am always amazed at just how beautiful our wonderful country is. When you take the time to look around, you notice many things you tend to forget in your busy day-to-day life.

Although cake decorating is nothing like driving in the countryside, I find it is ever-changing and can take on a life of its own. It is very easy to get engrossed in the decorating — many wonderful hours can go blissfully by where you are unaware of the outside world. I find it easy to zone out and enjoy the whole experience of creating something wonderful for a friend or loved one. What may start off as making a cake can very easily grow into a lifelong passion or mild obsession!

There is no gift more valuable than something you have made with love. It represents a moment in time that you dedicate to creating something for a special person. To see the expression on their face when you give your homemade masterpiece is priceless. There is no better feeling than when you realise you are creative, that the job wasn't that hard after all and that what you have made has brought so much pleasure to the person you created it for! And that is the reason I enjoy decorating so much. Not to say I don't have tears and tantrums when it doesn't go right!

Through these recipes I hope to pass on my love of and passion for our beautiful country and to inspire you to create some of my Kiwiana memories — or to create some of your own by taking the techniques and applying them to your own designs.

Enjoy this book — happy baking and, remember, you are only limited by your imagination.

*Kirsten Day*

# Hints and Tips

# Baking tips

- Temperatures given are for standard bake. If using a fan-forced oven, lower the temperature by 20°C.

- Read the recipe through so you understand the method first. This makes the process quicker.

- Before you start baking, get out all the ingredients. There is nothing worse than getting halfway through a recipe and finding you are out of an ingredient.

- Have the butter and eggs at room temperature. Butter will cream up much more easily if it is at room temperature, or softened.

- Unless making a sponge, use the flat paddle attachment of your mixer to cream butter.

- I like to use unsalted butter in my baking and certainly for making buttercream. This way you control how much salt goes into the cake. Salt also cuts the sweetness so by using unsalted butter you will get the full flavour of the buttercream.

- Crack eggs into a small dish before adding to the creamed butter and sugar. This will enable you to remove any shell that otherwise would end up in the cake batter. Also, if the egg is bad, you won't waste the butter.

- Always use fresh ingredients as if they are old, they will be less effective and your finished product may not be the best.

- Turn the oven on to the correct temperature before you begin to make the cake batter. That way it will be at the right temperature when the cakes go into the oven.

- Measuring the ingredients is key to ensuring a great finished product. Use measuring jugs, cups, spoons and scales.

- Watch you don't over-mix the cupcake batter. This will cause the cakes to be tough.

- Don't be tempted to open the oven door in the early minutes of cooking. The rush of cooler air will cause the cupcake batter to set and stop the cakes rising.

- Baking times are only a guide. Always test before removing from the oven. Check for other clues, such as the top springing back when lightly touched.

- Your raising agents have a shelf life! They will not last forever, so to get the best results keep an eye on how long you have had them. If it is over a year in the cupboard, it will be no good. Throw it out and get a new packet.

- Sugar syrup (see page 138) can be used to infuse flavour into cupcakes. Just drizzle a little over the top. Be careful not to add too much, or the cupcakes can become soggy.

- If you feel your cupcakes are a little overcooked when they come out of the oven, drizzle over a little sugar syrup to add some moisture back into them.

# Fondant

Fondant is a thick flavoured paste of sugar and water (see recipe on page 134), which is used to ice and decorate pastries, such as cupcakes, cake pops and whoopie pies. It can be purchased from cake specialty stores or online, and comes in many colours.

## Turning fondant into modelling paste

To create a stronger medium for making figurines, you will need to make a modelling paste. Modelling paste dries faster and more evenly and is stronger than fondant alone. It is very easy to make.

To fondant you need to add a hardening agent: either gum tragacanth — a natural gum powder; or tylose powder (CMC) — a manufactured version of gum tragacanth. Both will do the same job. I prefer to use tylose as it is much cheaper!

The amount of hardening agent needed to make your modelling paste depends on the temperature and the humidity levels. A rough guide is 1 teaspoon to 250 g fondant. As you do not always use a large quantity of modelling paste, you might need to play around with the amount of hardening agent you add. Be careful not to use too much tylose as this may cause your pieces to crack.

Knead the fondant until it is soft and pliable. Add the tylose and knead until it is well incorporated.

Any modelling paste that isn't being used should be wrapped tightly in plastic wrap and stored in an airtight container as it will dry quite quickly and become unusable.

## Storing fondant decorations

One of the great advantages of using fondant or modelling paste is that you can make your decorations well ahead of time and store them. I find creating the figurines or decorations takes the most time. Baking the cupcakes and popping the icing on top takes no time at all. If you have made the decorations ahead of time, your creations can be put together quickly.

Once you have made the decorations, place them in a cardboard cake box lined with baking paper, close the lid and put the box in a warm, dry spot until needed.

Do not store fondant decorations in an airtight container or in the fridge as the icing will draw in the moisture and cause your pieces to go sticky and spoil.

# How to form basic shapes

**Ball** — Every shape starts with a ball, which is then rolled into other shapes, such as apples, heads, etc.

**Log** — Take a ball shape and roll it between your palms to create a log shape. This shape is used for legs, arms, huhu grubs, gumboots, etc.

**Teardrop** — Take a ball shape and roll one half of it between your palms to narrow off one end, making a teardrop shape. This is used for bodies.

*TIP:* The head and body for a kiwi and a pukeko both start off as a teardrop shape, then the narrow end is rolled between the two index fingers to create a neck.

# How to colour icing

It is easier to colour sugar-based icings (like fondant) than butter-based ones (like buttercream). The fat in buttercream inhibits the absorption of the colour. You also use less colouring to colour fondant and royal icing than buttercream.

A concentrated colour gel or colour powder won't change the consistency of your icing, unlike liquid colours, and you will also get a much stronger colour. Liquid colours can cause fondant icing to get sticky. If this happens, add some icing sugar to the fondant to help absorb some of the stickiness.

To add colour to the icing, pick up a small amount of colour on a clean toothpick and add to the icing. Use a clean toothpick each time to ensure food particles or bacteria are not introduced to the icing colour, which can cause it to go off.

The colours will develop over time. It is a good idea to leave the icing for half an hour or so after colouring as the colour will deepen a shade or two on sitting.

Red and black — for any icings — are two tricky colours to make, and I'm not sure I have met anyone who hasn't had trouble with one or both of these colours. The secret that will ease the pain of colouring red and black is to follow a process. To make red, start by colouring the icing dark pink, then add red colouring. You still use a lot of colouring to make red but, by starting with pink, you will use a fraction of what you would need if you were starting with white icing. To make black, you need to start with brown chocolate icing, then add black colouring.

Buttercream made from real butter will create slightly different shades of colour as the butter has a yellow base. To get true colours it is best to use a vegetable shortening as the base as it yields an icing white in colour.

Don't be afraid to mix your colours to create brighter or unique shades to suit your design. Remember to always colour a little more icing than what you expect to need as you won't be able to match the colours again if you fall short and have to make more.

To get a marbled effect in your fondant, use a toothpick to add the colour, as described above, and partially knead. For a soft marbled effect, roll coloured fondant into a sausage shape. Lay the colours you wish to marble together and knead the fondant until the desired marbled effect is reached.

# Storing icing

- Butter-based buttercream should be stored in covered containers in the fridge. Bring the icing to room temperature before using. Beat the buttercream before using to make it light and fluffy again.
- Shortening-based buttercream is shelf stable and can be kept in the pantry in an airtight container.
- Royal icing is best kept in an airtight container and I always put a layer of plastic wrap on the top of the icing before putting on the lid. Royal icing goes hard when exposed to the air, rendering it no good to use.
- Cream cheese icing is best stored in the fridge in an airtight container.
- Chocolate ganache should be covered and stored in the fridge.
- Fondant icing should be wrapped tightly in plastic wrap and stored in an airtight container or snap-lock plastic bag in the pantry. It is not a good idea to store it in the fridge as it will draw in the moisture from the fridge and go sticky. Do not keep coloured fondant in direct light or the colours will fade.

## How to make edible glue

Sugar glue is very easy to make and will store in the fridge. You will need 1 tsp tylose powder (CMC) and 150 ml cooled boiled water. Mix the tylose powder and the water in a container. Put the lid on the container and give it a jolly good shake — don't worry if it looks a little lumpy. Leave it in the fridge overnight. The tylose will dissolve into a clear, thick gel. You can keep the glue in the fridge for up to two weeks.

*TIP:* Add a little more cooled boiled water if the glue gets too thick. A drop or two of white vinegar can be added to the glue to prevent contamination.
If you only require a small amount for a one-off job, reduce the recipe above to ¼ tsp tylose powder, and 35 ml cooled boiled water.

## How to make coloured sprinkles

It is so easy to make fantastic shades of sugar sprinkles using white nonpareils (available from cake-decorating shops and online). Add the nonpareils and a small amount of food powder dust or lustre dust to a snap-lock plastic bag and close the bag. Shake the bag well to evenly coat the sprinkles in the food powder. (It pays to start out with a little food powder and add more if you need to as it can easily become too dark.)

*TIP:* You can colour coconut and/or sugar in a similar way by placing in a snap-lock plastic bag, adding concentrated colour gel or paste, securing the top of the bag and massaging the colour through. Remember, though, that concentrated colours are just that: you only need a very small amount. If too much is used, the colour can come off on the mouths of unsuspecting cake-munchers. Although a great party trick, it may not be the experience you want for your guests. Less is best!

## How to fill a decorating bag with buttercream

This comes close to being one of the world's wonders! I have seen many different ways to tackle this job — some with success and others ending up (as many of you may relate to) in a sticky, delicious mess. Although I like to think 'you know you're doing it right if you're wearing it', it isn't always a great look! Here is the key and it's not hard.

Firstly, hold the narrow end of the decorating bag and fold the top of the bag down over your hand. Your hand will act as a support. You can use a glass instead of your hand if you need to be hands-free! Carefully spoon the icing into the bag no more than half full. Roll the top of the bag up, push the icing down and twist the top of the bag to prevent the icing coming up and out the top.

# How to pipe buttercream

Ensure the top of the bag is tightly wound off to avoid the icing from working its way up and out of the top.

To pipe the traditional high swirl on top, start with the bag at a 90-degree angle just above the outside edge of the cupcake and firmly squeeze the bag. Move the bag around the outside of the cupcake and, as you bring the icing higher, make the swirl smaller until you reach a point at the top.

To have the swirl flat, start with the bag at a 90-degree angle over the middle of the cupcake. Squeeze the icing out to attach to the top of the cupcake and move the bag out and around the centre to the outside edge.

Watch the pressure on the bag as you pipe. If you're not squeezing the bag firmly enough and moving the bag too quickly, the icing will stretch and break. The firmer the pressure, the faster the icing will come out. I think it is easier the faster you go. Take a deep breath and go for it and don't stop till you get to the top!

# How to melt chocolate

There are two ways to melt chocolate.

1. To melt chocolate on the stove top, you need:
- a small saucepan
- a glass or stainless steel mixing bowl
- chocolate, roughly chopped
- a metal spoon or silicon spatula

Bring a small amount of water to the boil in the saucepan. Once boiling, lower the temperature so the water is just simmering. If the water is still boiling when you put the bowl on top, pressure will build up under the bowl and water will spit out the sides of the bowl. If moisture gets into the chocolate, it will cause the chocolate to seize.

Place the bowl over the top of the saucepan, ensuring the bottom of the bowl doesn't touch the top of the water. If the bottom of the bowl is touching the top of the simmering water, the chocolate will overheat and seize.

Add the chocolate and stir as it melts. Once the chocolate has melted, turn off the heat and leave the bowl sitting on top of the saucepan.

2. To melt chocolate in the microwave, you need:
- chocolate, roughly chopped
- a microwave-proof bowl
- a silicon spatula

Put the chocolate in the bowl and heat in the microwave on a medium setting, checking every 30 seconds. Stir the chocolate each time you check to avoid hot spots or burning in the middle.

# Tools and Equipment

*The great thing about cake decorating is that you can build your tool kit slowly as your decorating skills grow. Many things around the kitchen can be used to cut, imprint and add detail to your designs. Below is a list of useful tools to start with.*

- **Rolling pin** — A small rolling pin is very useful when rolling small amounts of fondant.
- **Decorating bags** — There are several different types of decorating bag available on the market. When choosing a bag, consider the type of job. Paper or parchment decorating bags are good to use for small jobs, such as writing, or when working with royal icing or chocolate. Plastic disposable decorating bags are handy, as when the job is done you can simply remove the nozzle and throw away the bag. There can be a big difference between brands of bags. Buying good-quality bags from a cake speciality store will reduce the risk of having a disaster while decorating. Fabric bags are strong and reusable. They will last many years and buying a couple is a good investment.
- **Piping nozzles** — When starting to build your kit a large star nozzle is a must as it gives that common cupcake swirl we all know. A multi-opening nozzle is my favourite. You can use it for grass, hair, fur, seaweed, etc. Other useful nozzles are open star and plain round, of various sizes. These can be used to create mouths and smiles by gently pushing the curved edge onto a face and carefully rolling back and forth.
- **Coupler** — A coupler supports the nozzle at the end of the decorating bag, enabling the nozzle to be changed without having to first empty the bag. It will also hold the nozzle securely to the bag. To fit the coupler, remove the outside ring and drop the coupler into the decorating bag. Holding the edge of the coupler, cut off the end of the bag. Gently move the coupler into the end, pop on the nozzle and wind on the ring to hold the nozzle securely. Some couplers have nozzles that screw onto the end — these are fitted as above, then the nozzle is screwed onto the end of it.
- **Foam pieces** — Foam is especially useful for supporting fondant pieces as they dry, and for using under fondant petals as you press and move the veining tool to add detail to each petal.
- **Dusting puff/sugar shaker** — A dusting puff is a square of muslin filled with icing sugar, cornflour, or a mixture of both, then tied at the top. This is used to dust the work surface when rolling out fondant. The fine weave eliminates lumps and limits the quantity of sugar.
- **Paring knife** — A small paring knife is used to make neat, clean cuts through fondant. A knife with a thin blade is best. If the cuts are not clean, wash the knife as otherwise sugar will dry on the blade, causing the cuts to have a rough appearance. A serrated paring knife is useful if you need to shape the cupcake as for the kiwifruit (see page 36) and kiwi (see page 34).
- **Paintbrushes** — A range of art paintbrushes can be used to apply edible glue or dusting detail.
- **Scissors** — A small pair of scissors for cutting off the end of the decorating bag, cutting out templates and for general use.
- **Ruler** — Used to measure strips to ensure they are even. The edge of the ruler is used to imprint quilting lines, floor boards, etc.

# Kiwiana Cupcakes

# Ballet Slippers on Quilting Cupcakes

My parents would have loved me in these as a child, but I preferred the footwear on page 47!
*Makes 12*

12 lemon cupcakes (see page 95)

vanilla buttercream (see page 135)

fondant: 150 g white; 50 g pink

small rolling pin

dusting puff

plain round cutter (slightly smaller than the top of the cupcake)

small ruler

small palette knife

pearl-coloured sugar pearls

edible glue (see page 17)

small paintbrush

paring knife

1. Bake and cool cupcakes as per the recipe. Prepare the buttercream.
2. Spread a thin layer of buttercream over the top of each of the cupcakes.
3. Knead the white fondant until pliable and roll out to 5 mm thick. Dust the work surface if the icing is sticking. Be careful not to use too much as it will dry out the fondant.
4. Using the plain round cutter, cut a disc for each cupcake. Place the disc on the top of the cupcake and smooth out to the edge using your fingers. Smooth and polish by running the palm of your hand over the top.
5. To make the quilting design, push the edge of the small ruler or the edge of the palette knife into the fondant on top of the cupcake, leaving a 1 cm gap between each line. Turn the cupcake 90 degrees and repeat, indenting the lines. This will create the diamond pattern.
6. Where the lines intersect, attach a sugar pearl with a little dab of edible glue. Continue with the remaining cupcakes.
7. To make the slippers, roll equal pea-sized balls of pink fondant into short log shapes. Slightly narrow one end using your fingers. Place on the work surface and flatten slightly. Using the end of the paintbrush push down halfway into the slipper at the wide end to imprint the hole for the foot. You will need to do this several times to make the hole large enough. Roll and indent all the slippers — you will need two per cupcake.
8. Roll out a little pink fondant very thinly and cut long strips for the laces. Attach at the back of the slippers with a very short narrow strip. Use a little edible glue to fix the lace in place.
9. Position the slippers on top of each cupcake, attaching with a little glue on the sole of each slipper. Position the laces where you want them to sit and allow to dry.

*TIPS*
- These little slippers look lovely with a sprinkling of edible glitter over the top.
- Add lemon zest and a wee squeeze of lemon juice to flavour the buttercream.
- Add a tiny bow to the front of each slipper by piping on a little royal icing or buttercream with a very fine nozzle. Or roll fondant out and cut a very short, narrow strip, rolling the ends into the middle to create the bow loops and wrapping a short strip around the middle to hide the join. Attach to the top of each slipper with edible glue.

# Beehive Cupcakes

No unpleasant surprises when you disturb these beehives.
*Makes 12*

12 honey cupcakes (see page 94)

vanilla buttercream (see page 135)

black, yellow and green colour gel

dusting puff

small rolling pin

fondant: 50 g pink; 20 g red; 20 g black; 20 g white

small blossom cutter

small paintbrush

edible glue (see page 17)

sugar pearls

black edible food marker

small spatula

12 large marshmallows

couplers

piping bag

small round nozzle, large round nozzle and nozzle for grass (or multi-opening nozzle)

liquorice strap

15 orange jelly beans (some beehives can have two bees)

almond slices

① Bake and cool cupcakes as per the recipe. Prepare the buttercream by colouring 1 tbsp buttercream black and dividing the remaining buttercream evenly between two bowls. Colour one half yellow and the other green. Cover bowls of buttercream and set aside.

② Roll out pink fondant to 3 mm thick and, using the small blossom cutter, cut out 24 blossoms. Brush a little edible glue in the centre of each blossom and push in a sugar pearl.

③ To make the ladybirds, roll a small piece of the red fondant into a ball. Roll a smaller ball of black and attach to the red ball using a little edible glue. Roll two very small balls of white for the eyes and attach to the head. Use the edible food marker to draw in the pupils. Attach tiny black spots onto the ladybird's back. Set aside. Make a ladybird for each cupcake.

④ Using a spatula, spread a thin layer of green buttercream onto the top of each cupcake. Sit a large marshmallow on top of the buttercream. This will be the support for the beehive. Fit the coupler onto the end of the piping bag and attach the large round nozzle. Fill the piping bag with yellow buttercream. Holding your bag at a 90-degree angle, start piping around the base of the marshmallow and bring the spiral up to the top of the marshmallow without stopping squeezing. If you stop, the icing will stop coming out! If you get breaks in the piping, pop a bee on top of it and no one will ever know! Repeat with the remaining cupcakes.

⑤ Change to another piping bag (or clean out first bag), fit with a coupler and the nozzle for grass. Fill bag with green buttercream. Holding the tip close to but not touching the cupcake, squeeze out the icing to attach to the base of the beehive and outside edge of the cupcake. Keep squeezing for a moment as you pull the bag away from the cupcake. When you stop the pressure on the base, the icing will break off. The longer you squeeze the longer the grass! Pipe all the way around the base of the beehive. The grass can also cover any gaps. Repeat with the remaining cupcakes.

⑥ Cut a door for each beehive from the liquorice strap and push into the buttercream.

⑦ Place the blossoms and ladybirds around in the grass.

⑧ To make the bees, push orange jelly beans into the yellow wall of the beehive. Press an almond slice under each side of the jelly bean for wings. Use the black buttercream in a piping bag with the small round nozzle to pipe stripes and eyes on the jelly bean.

# Chocolate Christmas Pudding Cupcakes

Who said Christmas cake had to be made with fruit? If you are one of the growing group who isn't partial to a little slice of rich fruit cake, then this is a great cake for you. All the excitement of Christmas and in your flavour!
*Makes 12*

12 chocolate cupcakes (see page 90)

chocolate ganache (see page 131)

small round cake cards (to go under the cupcakes)

small palette knife

fondant: 250 g chocolate; 100 g white; 50 g green; 50 g red

dusting puff

small rolling pin

paring knife

paintbrush

edible glue (see page 17)

holly leaf cutter

1. Bake and cool cupcakes as per the recipe. Prepare the chocolate ganache.
2. Spread a little chocolate ganache onto the top of each cake card, peel the paper case off the cupcake, turn upside down and attach to the card.
3. Use the small palette knife to coat each of the cupcakes with a thin layer of ganache.
4. Knead the chocolate fondant until it is soft and pliable. Take a ball about the size of a golf ball and roll out to a circle with diameter 15 cm and about 3 mm thick. Lift onto the rolling pin and cover the entire cupcake. Gently smooth the fondant onto the cupcake, turning the cake as you smooth. Be careful not to stretch the fondant in a downward motion. This may cause it to tear on the top edge.
5. Once the fondant is attached and smooth all around, use a paring knife or spatula to trim around the bottom.
6. Knead the white icing until soft and pliable. Using a ball a little larger than a large marble, roll out to approximately 6 cm in diameter. Gently stretch out the fondant in random places to simulate runny icing. Brush a little edible glue on the top of the cupcake and lay the white fondant on top. Smooth it gently to attach and to soften the edges.
7. Roll out the green fondant and cut three holly leaves for each cupcake. Evenly place around the top of the cupcake and attach with edible glue.
8. Roll tiny red cherries using the red fondant and fix to the top of the holly leaves with edible glue.
9. Repeat for the remaining cupcakes.

*TIPS*
- Apply only a thin layer of ganache to the outside of the cake. If there is too much, it will move under the fondant creating lumps or, worse, will leak out from the bottom.
- If you have trouble finding small cake cards to go under the cakes, use a larger cake card and cut small discs out to the size you need.
- When using edible glue to attach fondant to fondant, you need only a very small amount. If you use too much glue, the pieces will become very sticky and may even slide down the cake. Not a good look!

# Chocolate Kiwi Cupcakes

These are a fun little kiwi to make. Try them in different colours — pink looks really cute!
*Makes 12*

12 standard chocolate cupcakes (see page 90)

12 mini chocolate cupcakes (as above)

chocolate buttercream (see page 135)

coupler

piping bag

nozzle for grass

dusting puff

small rolling pin

fondant: 20 g white; 20 g black; 50 g orange; 10 g green; 10 g pink

black edible food marker

small paintbrush

paring knife

edible glue (see page 17)

1. Bake and cool cupcakes as per the recipe. Prepare the buttercream.

2. Remove the cupcake case from a mini cupcake. Turn the cupcake upside down and place it slightly off-centre on top of a standard cupcake. Attach with a small amount of chocolate buttercream. Repeat until all the mini cupcakes are attached to the tops of the standard cupcakes.

3. Fit the coupler to the piping bag and attach the nozzle. Fill the bag with chocolate buttercream.

4. To pipe the feathers, start at the edge of the standard cupcake. Hold the nozzle close to but not touching the cupcake and apply pressure to the bag. Reduce the pressure as you pull the bag away from the cake; this will cause the icing to stop coming out of the bag and break off. Continue all around the cupcake and up and over the top of the mini cupcake.

5. Roll out two half pea-sized balls of white fondant and place on the face for the eyes. Using the marker, draw in the eye detail. Roll a small amount of the black fondant into a short log shape and then roll the ends to make a point. Curl slightly and place over the top of the eye for the eyebrows.

6. To make the beak, roll a small pea-sized ball of orange fondant into a long teardrop shape. Flatten slightly. Push to attach between the eyes and indent two holes for the nose using the end of a paintbrush.

7. To make the feet, flatten two small balls of orange fondant and cut a 'V' shape for the toes. Using your fingers, smooth the cut edge and roll the tip of each toe into a point. Pinch the heel into a point. Attach the feet to the front of the cupcake by placing them into the buttercream. Repeat to make 12 kiwis.

8. To make the hat, roll a pea-sized ball of green fondant and flatten by pushing flat with your finger. Roll another small amount of green and a small amount of black together to create a marble effect. Roll into a ball and flatten on one side. Attach to the top of the green disc with a little edible glue. Roll a tiny ball for the button on the top and attach. Place on top of the kiwi's head.

9. To make the bow, roll a small amount of pink fondant to 3 mm thick. Cut a thin strip approx 3 cm long and ½ cm wide. Turn the strip over and roll both ends into the centre and glue to attach. Cut a short strip the same width but only 1 cm long. Lay this strip over the top of the join and wrap underneath. Give the middle of the bow a bit of a pinch to shape, and place on the kiwi's head.

# Chocolate Kiwifruit Cupcakes

Add a little dried kiwifruit powder to the green buttercream to add a flavour surprise!
*Makes 18*

18 green vanilla cupcakes (see page 99)

chocolate buttercream (see page 135)

dusting puff

small rolling pin

fondant: 100 g green; 50 g white

60 mm round cutter; 20 mm round cutter

small paintbrush

edible glue (see page 17)

chocolate sprinkles

black edible food marker

1. Bake and cool cupcakes as per the recipe. Prepare chocolate buttercream.

2. Remove the cupcake cases from six of the cupcakes and cut in half vertically.

3. Cover the top of each remaining cupcake with chocolate buttercream. Sit a half cupcake, cut-side down, on top of the cupcake. Trim the back of the attached cupcake so it is a rounded shape. Spread a thin layer of chocolate buttercream across the front of the cupcake.

4. Roll out the green fondant to 3 mm thick. Using a 60 mm round cutter, cut out a disc and place it on the front of the cupcake. This is the inside of the cut kiwifruit. Gently smooth the icing into the crease and along both sides. Take a small ball of white fondant and a small ball of green. Gently knead them together to create a subtle marbled effect. Roll out to 3 mm thick and cut out a 20 mm disc. Dab a little edible glue onto the back and attach to the centre of the cupcake. Smooth around the outside edge.

5. Spread a thin layer of chocolate buttercream over the back and sides of the cupcake and roll gently in the chocolate sprinkles.

6. Draw in the seed detail using the edible food marker.

7. Repeat with the remaining cupcakes.

*TIP*
- To flavour these cupcakes add 2 tbsp dried kiwifruit powder to the vanilla cupcake recipe. Dried fruit powders are available from specialty food stores.

# Easter Bunny and Bunnies Down the Hole Cupcakes

A few little bunnies hopping down into a hole give these cupcakes character, and carrot cupcakes make a nice change to all the chocolate at Easter-time.
*Makes 12*

12 carrot cupcakes (see page 93)

cream cheese icing (see page 136)

1 tsp tylose powder (CMC)

fondant: 200 g white; 150 g orange; 50 g green; 50 g pink

paring knife

small paintbrush

edible glue (see page 17)

dusting puff

small rolling pin

black edible food marker

toothpick

short length of uncooked spaghetti

large open star nozzle

piping bag

green colour gel

nozzle for grass

1. Bake and cool cupcakes, and prepare cream cheese icing. Set aside.

2. Add tylose to 150 g white fondant and knead in well.

3. To make a bunny, roll a ball of white fondant into a teardrop shape for the body. Two small pea-sized balls flattened on one side will become the feet. Using the back of the paring knife, indent the front of each ball for the toes. Sit the flattened side underneath the body and attach with a little edible glue. Take a piece of fondant the size of a large marble and roll into a log shape. The arms are a log shape, narrowed slightly at each end for the wrists. Do this by rolling each end between your two index fingers. Flatten both ends with your fingers to form the hands and use the paring knife to mark on the fingers. Wrap the arms around the top of the body and attach with glue. Roll a marble-sized piece of white fondant for the head into a ball.

4. Slightly indent along the front of the face where the eyes are going to give the face a little shape. Use the back of the paintbrush to make the two eye indentations. Roll a tiny ball of white fondant and pop into each hole for the eyes. The black food marker will add the eye detail.

5. The ears are two pea-sized balls of white fondant flattened between your fingers and gently pulled into the shape and size needed. Repeat the same process, just smaller, with the pink fondant and glue to the inside of the ear. Attach to the back of the head.

6. Two small balls, flattened a little for the cheeks, are placed below the eyes and textured with the end of a toothpick. A tiny ball of pink fondant for the nose is placed above the middle of the cheeks. Push the uncooked spaghetti down through the body from the top, cut off about 1 cm above the top of the body, brush a little glue around the top of the body where the head will attach, and slide the head down the spaghetti and press gently to fix to the body. The spaghetti will act as support as the body dries. Roll a little ball of white for the pompom tail at the back, and attach with glue.

7. Fit the coupler and large open star nozzle to the piping bag and fill with cream cheese icing. Pipe a flat swirl by starting to pipe from the centre and swirling to the outside. Sit the bunny on top.

**8** To make the carrots, roll orange fondant into small balls, then into teardrop shapes. Push the end of the paintbrush into the wide end for the carrot top to go. Roll a small ball of green fondant into a thin log shape and make a cut approximately 1 cm at one end. Gently roll the cut edges; this will become the carrot top. Brush a little glue into the hole at the top of each carrot and insert the top. Use the back of the paring knife to make the impressions on the carrots. Allow to dry. Glue in place.

**9** The rabbit 'bottoms' are large marble-sized balls of white fondant rolled and flattened at the base. To do this place the ball onto the work surface and gently smooth over the top down to the bottom. The icing will take on a rounded disk shape. Roll a pea-sized ball for the tail and push the end of the toothpick into the icing to give it texture. The feet are two pea-sized balls rolled into a slight log shape and flattened. Two balls of flattened pink fondant attached to the sole of the foot become the pads. Tiny balls for the toes are the last detail to add; brush a little glue to attach the feet.

**10** Colour up some cream cheese icing with a small amount of green colour gel. Fit the nozzle for grass to the end of the bag and fill with the green cream cheese icing. Pipe the grass onto the top of the cupcake by holding the bag close to the cupcake and applying pressure. Reduce the pressure as you bring the bag away from the cupcake, causing it to break off. Place a rabbit bottom in the middle of the grass and pop some carrots around.

*TIPS*
- Add tylose powder to the white fondant, particularly if the weather is humid. This will help the figurine to dry.
- Remember that once you add the tylose powder to the fondant it will start to dry. Ensure you keep any modelling paste covered and airtight when not using it.
- If your bunny starts to lean backwards while drying, roll a small ball of fondant and attach underneath to prop him back up.
- I tend to support any upright figurines while they dry. Place a can or glass behind them overnight — that way they won't start to lean backwards. Getting up in the morning after a long night modelling only to find your creations all curled over can be very upsetting!

# Tomato Sauce Bottle Cupcakes and Fish and Chips Cupcakes

Many a gorgeous evening in New Zealand is spent on the beach eating fish and chips. The tomato sauce bottle is a must!

## Tomato Sauce Bottle Cupcakes
*Makes 12*

12 red velvet cupcakes (see page 97)

chocolate buttercream (see page 135)

small spatula

fondant: 100 g green; 100 g red

dusting puff

small rolling pin

plain round cutter (slightly smaller than the top of the cupcake)

small open star nozzle

small calyx cutter

small paintbrush

edible glue (see page 17)

toothpick

1. Bake and cool cupcakes as per the recipe. Prepare the buttercream.

2. Using the spatula spread a little buttercream over the top of the cupcakes.

3. Knead the green fondant until it is soft and pliable. Roll out to 5 mm thick. Use the round cutter to cut out a disc for the top of the cupcake. Place the fondant disc on the cupcake and gently stretch the fondant out to the edge by smoothing it from the middle out. It is much easier to use a smaller cutter and smooth it out than having the disc too large and having to shrink it.

4. Once the icing is on top of the cupcake and smooth it is time to create the grass effect. Push the points of the open star nozzle into the fondant, creating a rough texture.

5. To make the tomato sauce bottle, knead the red fondant until it is soft and pliable. Divide the fondant into balls a little larger than a marble. Place the balls you're not using under plastic wrap, so they don't dry out.

6. Roll the red fondant into a smooth ball. Roll out the green fondant to 3 mm thick and use the calyx cutter to cut out the top of the tomato. Trim off the points and carefully soften the edges. Attach to the top of the red ball with a little edible glue.

7. Use a toothpick to make impressions around the top of the bottle. Start at the top and gently press the toothpick into the icing and move the toothpick down a little.

8. Roll a very small ball of green fondant into a log and glue onto the top of the tomato. Carefully press the end of the paintbrush into the top for the spout.

9. To create the tomato sauce on the outside of the bottle, roll a little red fondant and pop into the spout. Make a couple of tiny teardrop shapes for the sides of the spout and down the bottle. Repeat to make 12 bottles. Attach the bottle to the top of the cupcake with a little glue.

*TIP*
- The way to get all the bottles an even size is to weigh the balls as you divide up the icing.

# Fish and Chips Cupcakes
*Makes 12*

12 chocolate cupcakes (see page 90)

chocolate buttercream (see page 135)

small spatula

fondant: 200 g green; 150 g white; 20 g red

dusting puff

small rolling pin

plain round cutter (slightly smaller than the top of the cupcake)

small open star nozzle

black edible food marker

edible glue (see page 17)

small paintbrush

brown colour gel

palette knife

1. Bake and cool cupcakes as per the recipe. Prepare the buttercream.

2. Using the spatula, cover the top of each cupcake with chocolate buttercream.

3. Knead the green fondant until soft, roll out to 5 mm thick and cut out disc using the plain round cutter. Place on top of each cupcake and smooth out to the edge as for the Tomato Sauce Bottle cupcakes. Using the star nozzle, push the points into the fondant to give texture and the effect of grass. Repeat with the remaining cupcakes and set aside.

4. For the newspaper, roll out a little ball of white fondant to 3 mm thick. Cut out a square. Write in the newspaper heading and the news using the food marker. Be careful not to press too hard or you will drag on the icing.

5. Place a smaller square of white fondant on an angle on top of the newspaper, attach with glue.

6. Adding a tiny amount of brown colour gel to a small ball of fondant will give you the colour for the chips. Roll icing out thin and cut the chips with the edge of the palette knife. Add a little more colour to the off-white offcuts and mould into a piece of fish. Glue the fish and chips to the paper. Lastly, mould a small piece of red fondant for the sauce and place on the side using a little glue.

# Gumboot Cupcakes

There isn't one of us who hasn't jumped in a mud puddle at some time. It always seems like a great idea — until your boots fill up with water!
*Makes 12*

12 chocolate mud cupcakes (see page 92)

chocolate buttercream (see page 135)

fondant: 50 g black; 10 g red; 50 g pink; 10 g white

small spatula

ball tool

dusting puff

small rolling pin

small blossom cutter

small paintbrush

edible glue (see page 17)

yellow edible food marker

❶ Bake and cool cupcakes as per the recipe. Prepare chocolate buttercream.

❷ To make the red band gumboots, roll black fondant into a ball about the size of a small marble. Roll the ball into a log shape approximately 2 cm long. Stand the log upright and gently start to pull the front of the bottom end out to create the toe of the boot. Pull gently, smoothing the icing as you go. Once the toe is pulled out you have the basic shape of the boot. Hold the boot upside down and push the side of the spatula across the sole to mark the heel. Gently narrow the point where the heel is marked.

❸ Carefully hollow the top of the boot using the ball tool. Press the tool down and gently turn in a circular motion to create the opening of the boot. Roll out the red fondant into thin strips to attach the detail using a little glue. Start with the strip around the bottom of the boot, then the top. A small red square is placed in the front at the top of each boot. Repeat to complete the required number of boots.

❹ The pink boots are made in the same way as the red band gumboots, only they have flowers as the detail. To make the flowers, roll out the white fondant. Use the dusting puff if the fondant is sticking. Cut out the blossom shape with a small cutter and attach to the boot with a little edible glue. Using the food marker, dot a little yellow spot into the centre of each blossom. Repeat to complete the required number of boots.

❺ Using a small spatula, place a good amount of buttercream on top of each cupcake and spread carefully out to the edge. Add a little more buttercream if you think it needs it. With the flat side of the spatula, press down on the top of the buttercream and pull up. This will add texture and create peaks in the buttercream.

❻ Put a pair of boots on top. They will stick into the buttercream.

*TIPS*
- Change the colour of the boots to personalise and create your own look. City boots or country boots, you are in charge of the design!
- Paint a design onto the boots using diluted colour paste. Dilute the colour using clear alcohol.
- Use different-shaped cutters, such as stars, etc.
- To add more detail, pipe blobs of chocolate buttercream onto the boots so it looks like the mud has splashed onto them.

# Hedgehog Cupcakes

My mother's nickname was 'Hedgehog', given to her by her sister 'Frog'. Mum was always so excited when the hedgehogs came out at night and we would be dragged out to see them. She would feed them cat food (I'm not sure how the cat felt about having his bowl whipped outside to feed the hedgehogs). This one's for you, Mum!

*Makes 12*

12 chocolate cupcakes (see page 90)

chocolate buttercream (see page 135)

vanilla buttercream (see page 135)

black and green colour gel

coupler

piping bag

small round nozzle and nozzle for grass

12 Hershey's Kisses, foil removed

12 Cadbury Snowballs

dusting puff

small rolling pin

fondant: 10 g pink; 10 g yellow; 20 g red; 20 g black; 10 g white

small flower/blossom cutters

small paintbrush

edible glue (see page 17)

sugar pearls

black edible food marker

1. Bake and cool cupcakes as per the recipe. Prepare chocolate and vanilla buttercreams.

2. Colour 2 tbsp chocolate buttercream black and set aside. Attach the coupler to the end of the piping bag and fit the nozzle for grass. Fill with vanilla buttercream coloured green. Set aside.

3. Hold the tip close to but not touching the top of the cupcake. Squeeze the bag and as the icing comes out ensure it attaches to the cupcake before pulling away slowly and releasing the pressure, causing the icing to stop coming out and break off. Pipe grass over the tops of all the cupcakes.

4. Clean piping bag and tip and refill with the chocolate buttercream.

5. To make the hedgehogs, put a little chocolate buttercream onto the bottom of a Hershey's Kiss and attach to the side of a Snowball. This forms the head and body. Pipe the prickles around the sides of the Snowball with chocolate buttercream, using the same technique you used for the grass on the cupcakes. The coconut can give you a run for your money, causing the prickles to sometimes fall off, so make sure you use good pressure to force the buttercream to attach. Place the hedgehog on the top of the cupcake, then continue to pipe the rest of the prickles over the sides and top.

6. Pipe the eyes and nose using the black buttercream and a small round piping tip. Repeat to make 12 hedgehogs.

7. Dust the bench with the dusting puff and roll out the pink fondant to 3 mm thick. Cut out flowers and blossoms using the cutters. Dab a little edible glue in the centre and pop on sugar pearls. Repeat with the remaining pink and yellow fondant.

8. Place the flowers in the grass and on the heads of some hedgehogs. To make ladybirds, see page 30.

*TIPS*
- I have made these for SPCA Cupcake Day for several years now. They are a lot of fun and you can dress them up as much as you want, e.g. hats for boys and bows for girls.
- Colour the prickles any colour you like; they look pretty groovy in pink and purple!
- Mix and match with the sunflowers cupcakes (see page 82) to create a garden scene.
- If you want to make a family of hedgehogs, use a Malteser for the body and a chocolate drop for the nose. How cute is that mini hedgehog?

# Huhu Grub Cupcakes

This is one of my favourite cupcakes. Nothing says you are a Kiwi more than eating a huhu grub. This is a more pleasant way of doing it.
*Makes 12*

12 peanut butter cupcakes (see page 96)

peanut butter buttercream (see recipe page 135)

large open star nozzle

piping bag

fondant: 100 g white; 10 g black; 50 g green

small paintbrush

edible glue (see page 17)

small rolling pin

black edible food marker

dusting puff

leaf cutter

thin modelling foam

veining tool

chocolate Flake bar, cut into thin short logs, or roughly grated chocolate

1. Bake and cool cupcakes as per the recipe. Prepare the buttercream.
2. Fit the large open star nozzle into the piping bag and fill with the peanut butter buttercream.
3. To pipe the swirl on top of the cupcake, hold the bag at a 90-degree angle in the middle of the cupcake. Apply pressure to the piping bag and, as the icing comes out, swirl from the middle around to the outside edge. Starting your swirl from the middle keeps the icing flat. Repeat with the remaining cupcakes.
4. To make the grubs, knead the white fondant until workable and divide into 12 even marble-sized balls. Cover with a little plastic wrap to prevent them drying out. To shape the grub, roll a ball into a log shape approximately 3 cm long. Roll the log between the outside edges of your index fingers to shape the neck and body indentations.
5. Roll tiny balls of black fondant for the eyes and attach with edible glue. Put a tiny fleck of white fondant into the corner of the eye, then mark pupils with black edible marker.
6. Knead the green fondant until soft and pliable and roll out to 3 mm thick. Dust the work surface if the icing is sticking. Cut out 6 leaves and place on thin modelling foam. Use the veining tool to run a line down the centre of the leaf and then angle veins from the outside edge to the middle. Gently shape the leaves by pinching the base and twisting the top slightly.
7. Evenly place 3 of the leaves around the top of the cupcake. Place 3 chocolate logs over the top of the leaves. Place another leaf over the top of each chocolate log join. This will cover the point where the logs meet.
8. Sit the grub in the centre, using a little glue, if necessary.
9. Repeat to make 12 grubs and decorate the remaining cupcakes.

*TIPS*
- You can dust a little pink lustre dust onto the grub's cheeks if you want to add a little more detail.
- A tiny hat for the grub's head would be really cute! Too easy — roll a small ball of coloured fondant and flatten between your fingers and thumb. Roll another ball and attach to the top of the flat disc. Gently smooth the top ball down to meet the outside edge of the flat disc. Pop a tiny ball on top.

# Jaffa, Snifter and Pineapple Lump Cupcakes

These have to be my favourite three sweets. When I made these into cupcakes they were a huge hit with everyone. The Snifter cupcakes were the most popular, but unfortunately you can't buy Snifters any more.
*Makes 12*

12 chocolate cupcakes (see page 90)

vanilla buttercream (see page 135)

chocolate buttercream (see page 135)

red, green and yellow colour gel

orange, spearmint and pineapple essence

large open star nozzle

piping bag

small spatula

1. Bake and cool cupcakes as per the recipe. Prepare vanilla and chocolate buttercreams.

2. Divide the vanilla buttercream into three bowls. Colour one red and flavour orange, colour the next green and flavour spearmint, and colour the final yellow and flavour pineapple.

3. Fit the star nozzle into the end of the piping bag. Fold the piping bag over and, using the spatula, push chocolate buttercream along both sides of the inside of the bag. Then fill with the red buttercream. Push the icing in the middle down towards the narrow end first before pushing both sides down. Wind the top to secure the icing in the bag.

4. Holding the bag at a 90-degree angle to the cupcake and starting at the outside edge, begin to apply pressure. As the icing comes out, move the bag around the cupcake, reducing the size of the swirl as you move up the cupcake. You are in control of your decorating bag. If you only want a little icing, start your swirl a little in from the edge and bring it into the centre more quickly. Repeat the above technique to make three more jaffa cupcakes.

5. Clean out the piping bag and nozzle and repeat the technique to make four of each cupcake with the remaining coloured and flavoured icings.

*TIPS*
- *If the bag is wound tightly at the top, you don't have to put as much pressure on to get the icing out. It will also stop any icing coming out the top of the bag.*
- *Remember when piping a swirl on top of the cupcake, if you stop applying pressure, the icing will stop coming out and you will get a break in the swirl. So take a deep breath and go for it!*
- *Although, sadly, we are no longer able to buy Snifters (you could try mint-flavoured lollies), you can garnish the jaffa cupcakes with Jaffas and the pineapple cupcakes with Pineapple Lumps.*

# Jandal Cupcakes

Jandals are a Kiwi icon — everyone has a favourite pair. The design on these jandals is up to you.
*Makes 12*

12 vanilla cupcakes (see page 99)

vanilla buttercream (see page 135)

green colour gel

coupler

piping bag

nozzle for grass

fondant: 200 g of colours of your choice

dusting puff

small rolling pin

small round or oval cutter

paintbrush

edible glue (see page 17)

decorations for jandals (see Tips on page 55)

1. Bake and cool cupcakes as per the recipe. Prepare the buttercream by adding green colour gel and mixing thoroughly.

2. Fit the coupler to the end of the piping bag and attach the multi-opening nozzle. Fill piping bag with green buttercream. Set aside.

3. To make the jandals, knead the fondant until soft and lightly dust the work surface with the dusting puff. Roll out fondant to 3 mm thick. Cut out the fondant using a round or oval cutter. If using a round cutter, gently stretch into an oval shape slightly narrower at the heel end. An oval cutter just requires narrowing at one end.

4. Using the end of the paintbrush, make three indents on the jandal — one at the toe and two a third of the way down on each side. The jandal straps will attach to these. Add a little glue to the inside of each indent.

5. Roll a pea-sized amount of fondant into a ball, cut in half and roll each into a long log. Flatten the log using your finger, fold in half lengthwise, keeping the two ends separate (your jandal straps will look like the letter Y) and cut to the right length. Carefully roll the three ends into points and insert the jandal straps into the holes. Trim the ends of the straps again, if needed, to achieve the right length.

6. Repeat with the remaining fondant. You will need two jandals per cupcake.

7. To pipe the grass on the top of each cupcake, hold the bag close to but not touching the cupcake and apply pressure to the bag. As the buttercream comes out make sure the icing attaches to the top of the cupcake. Pull the bag away while reducing the pressure on the bag. This will cause the buttercream to stop coming out of the bag and to break off, creating the grass effect. I like to start by going all the way around the outside, working my way into the middle. Cover all the cupcakes with grass.

8. Sit the jandals on top of the cupcakes.

*TIPS*

How you decorate your jandals is up to you. The jandals in the image are decorated as follows:

- Black — the writing is painted on using silver edible paint, and a red heart sprinkle.
- Pohutukawa flowers — roll out a small amount of white fondant to 3 mm thick. Roll tiny amounts of red fondant into balls and flatten between your finger and thumb. Cut the discs into quarters and place randomly on top of the white fondant. Gently press tiny green balls of fondant at the pointed end of the red flower. Using the small rolling pin, carefully roll over the top. This will roll the three colours together. Use gold edible paint to make small dots at the top of each flower.
- New Zealand flag — cut out strips of white and red fondant to create the Union Jack and attach with edible glue, and use small star cutters for the stars.
- If you would like your jandals on the beach, cover the tops of the cupcakes with uncoloured buttercream or caramel buttercream (see page 130) and roll carefully in brown sugar. You may need to sprinkle the brown sugar over the top to get the best coverage.
- You can place tiny flowers around the jandals to add a little something extra.

# Kiwi on Blossom with Fern Cupcakes

You won't have to wait till night-time for these fellows to come out!
*Makes 12*

12 vanilla cupcakes (see page 99)

vanilla buttercream (see page 135)

green colour gel

small spatula

fondant: 150 g green; 50 g orange; 50 g white; 50 g black; 150 g brown/chocolate; 20 g yellow

dusting puff

small rolling pin

plain round cutter (slightly smaller than the top of the cupcake)

5 petal blossom cutter

small paintbrush

edible glue (see page 17)

¼ tsp tylose powder (CMC)

silicone fern mould

silver edible paint

black edible food marker

paring knife

coupler

nozzle for grass

piping bag

1. Bake and cool cupcakes as per the recipe. Prepare the buttercream.

2. Colour the vanilla buttercream by adding green colour gel and mixing thoroughly. Using a small spatula, spread a little buttercream over the tops of the cupcakes.

3. Knead the green fondant until soft and pliable. Dust the work surface with the dusting puff to prevent the icing sticking as you roll. Roll the fondant out to 5 mm thick. Using the plain round cutter, cut out 12 discs to cover the top of each cupcake. Place the disc on the top and gently push the icing out to the edge. Smooth the top with the palm of your hand. Cover the remaining cupcakes.

4. Soften and roll out the orange fondant to 3 mm thick. Cut out a flower using the 5 petal blossom cutter. Brush lightly on the base with edible glue and place on the top of the cupcake. Repeat with remaining cupcakes.

5. Colour a golf ball-sized piece of white fondant grey by kneading a very small piece of black into it. Add tylose powder to the ball and knead in well to make modelling paste.

6. Very lightly dust the silicon fern mould with the dusting puff. Push a small ball of grey fondant into the cavity of the mould. Trim off any excess icing with a spatula. Smooth with your fingers. Bend the mould back slightly and the icing will come free. Gently remove from the mould and put onto a lightly dusted work surface to dry. Continue to make all the ferns.

7. Once all the ferns are made, each needs to be painted silver. The paint won't take long to dry so if you feel it needs two coats, go for it!

8. To make the kiwi, roll a piece of brown fondant a little larger than a large marble into a ball. Roll one end of the ball to create a teardrop shape. The narrow end will become the head. About 1 cm below the top, softly roll the teardrop between your two index fingers to indent slightly for the neck area.

9. The eyes are two small round balls of white fondant; draw black detail onto the eyes with the edible food marker. To give the kiwi eyebrows, roll a tiny ball of brown fondant into a log, then roll each end to create a point. Curve slightly and attach to the top of the eyes.

**⑩** The beak is a small piece of yellow fondant rolled into a long log shape. Roll one end into a point. Attach to the kiwi's face between the eyes.

**⑪** Roll two pea-sized balls of yellow fondant into a log shape for the legs. Join the legs at one end and set on top of the cupcake, coming out over two of the petals. Attach the legs to the petal using a little edible glue. The boots are made by rolling two small marble-sized pieces of black fondant into a short log shape. Stand the log upright and gently begin to pull the front of the boot out. Hold the boot up and use the back of the paring knife to indent for the heel; squeeze the sides of the boot slightly to give it shape. Attach to the end of the legs.

**⑫** Brush a little glue on the top of the flower and sit the kiwi on top of the legs. The body will hide the join where the legs meet.

**⑬** To make the wings, roll two marble-sized balls of brown fondant into a teardrop shape, then flatten between your fingers. Give the bottom of each wing some feathering by running the knife down around the bottom edge of the wing. Position the wings where you want them. Where the wing meets the body, add a very small dot of glue to fix in place. Sit the fern upright under one wing, attaching with a little glue. Repeat to make 12 kiwis.

**⑭** Fit the coupler and the nozzle to the end of the piping bag and fill with the green buttercream. Hold the bag close to but not touching the edge of the cupcake and apply pressure to the bag. As the icing starts to come out make sure it attaches to the cupcake and move the bag away from the cupcake. As you reduce the pressure on the bag, the icing will stop coming out and it will break off, creating the grass effect. Run the grass all the way around the cupcake. Repeat for the remaining cupcakes.

*TIPS*
- When rolling fondant into a ball, push the ball flat between your hands and, as you start the rolling, slowly start to cup your hands. This will remove any cracks or lines in the fondant. If you find there are lines in the ball, flatten and start the rolling process again.
- When painting fondant silver, it is a good idea to first colour the fondant grey. That way if you miss a spot or don't get a great coverage with the paint, it won't show so much.
- When mixing white and coloured fondant, it is a good idea to take a very small amount of the coloured fondant and add to the white. Keep adding small quantities of the coloured fondant until you get the colour you wish.
- Adding tylose powder to the fondant will make the fondant stiffer to work with and it will dry much faster than fondant alone. Keep any icing that isn't being used under plastic wrap to prevent it drying out. It is easier to get your pieces out of a silicone mould if the fondant has tylose powder added; otherwise it can be too soft and therefore difficult to remove.
- Watch that you don't dust too much icing sugar into the silicone moulds as you will lose a lot of the detail.

# Marshmallow Sheep Cupcakes

There are many different types of sheep here in New Zealand and they come in many different colours — even pink!
*Makes 12*

12 vanilla cupcakes (see page 99)

vanilla buttercream (see page 135)

fondant: 150 g ivory; 50 g white; 50 g pink

small paintbrush

black edible food marker

edible glue (see page 17)

piping nozzle or small round cutter

pink and white mini marshmallows

small rolling pin

dusting puff

small spatula

1. Bake and cool cupcakes as per the recipe. Prepare the buttercream.
2. To make the sheep's head, roll a piece of the ivory fondant into a ball, then slightly elongate. Using the side of your little finger, gently make an impression where the eyes are to go. Make a small impression using the end of the paintbrush for the eyes. Roll two very small balls of white fondant and sit them in the impressions. Put in pupil detail using the food marker.
3. To make the ears, roll two small balls of ivory fondant into a teardrop shape and flatten between your fingers. Do the same with the pink fondant, slightly smaller, and attach to one side of each ivory shape. Fix the ears to the head pink side-down with a little edible glue.
4. To make the mouth, roll the wide end of a piping nozzle or small round cutter into the end of the head. For the nostrils, make two small indents above the mouth with the end of the paintbrush.
5. To make a bow for the top of the head, roll out pink fondant and cut a very thin strip. Roll the ends into the middle. Wrap a very small, thin strip around the middle to cover the joins. Attach to the head with a little edible glue.
6. Repeat to make 12 heads.
7. Using a spatula, spread buttercream over the top of the cupcake and position the head. Attach the mini marshmallows for the body by pushing them into the buttercream. Place them really close together.
8. Repeat with the remaining cupcakes.

*TIPS*
- You can make marshmallow sheep with mini cupcakes too; just make the heads smaller.
- You can have some fun with these by mixing up your colours. Create white sheep with black heads by using black fondant to make the head.
- Create a wonderful scene by setting up a wire cupcake stand (can be purchased or hired from a cake specialty store) and putting green tissue up in between the arms. Then when the cupcakes are on the stand it will look as if the sheep are on a hillside paddock.

# Mini Present Cupcakes

Homemade edible gifts are the greatest to receive. These little cakes can be made well ahead of time by using fruit cake. By changing the pattern on the cakes they can be tailored to any occasion.
*Makes 12*

12 small square cakes (see Tips on page 64 and recipes on pages 114–117)

vanilla buttercream (see page 135)

small spatula

fondant: 150 g white; 150 g red; 150 g green

dusting puff

small rolling pin

paring knife

paintbrush

edible glue (see page 17)

¼ tsp tylose powder (CMC)

paper towel

small star cutters

edible glitter

1. Bake and cool cakes as per the recipe. Prepare the buttercream.

2. Using the spatula, cover each cake with buttercream.

3. Knead the white fondant until soft and pliable. Divide the fondant into four equal balls. Cover three with plastic wrap and roll out the remaining ball to 5 mm thick.

4. Lift the fondant and cover one cake. Gently smooth the icing, pushing it into the sides of the cake to prevent it from stretching. Trim around the bottom and set aside. I like to start with all the white cakes before I bring out the coloured fondant. This prevents the coloured fondant getting onto the white.

5. Repeat with the remaining cakes.

6. Roll out a contrasting strip approximately 2½ cm wide for the ribbon. Place over the top of each cake and attach with a little edible glue.

7. To make the bow, add tylose powder to one of the remaining fondant colours and knead the powder in well. This will make the fondant harden quickly and hold its shape. Keep all fondant covered when not using as it will start to dry, causing cracking. Roll out the fondant to approximately 3 mm thick. Cut a strip about 8 cm long and 2½ cm wide. Gently gather the ends and roll into the middle. Attach the ends to the middle with edible glue. Support the loops by rolling a small piece of paper towel and placing inside each loop. Remove the paper once the loops have hardened. Cut a much shorter strip and roll around the middle of the bow. The ribbon tassles are cut the same width as the bow loops. Trim one end by cutting out a 'V' and gather the other end. Glue the gathered end to the top of the cake. Pop a spot of glue part way down on the underside of the ribbon and attach to the cake. Brush the bottom of the bow with edible glue and sit it on top of the cake to cover the gathered ends of the tassles. Repeat with the remaining fondant colours and cakes.

8. Using small star cutters, cut out stars from the remaining fondant and attach to the cake using the edible glue.

### TIPS
- If you do not have a tin that bakes small square cakes, cut a 20 cm cake into nine portions.
- These little cakes make great gifts. Pop them onto a small cake card and wrap with cellophane. A lovely Christmas ribbon and they're all done! If you really want to get ahead for Christmas, make fruit cakes (see page 117), then they can be made well ahead of time and stored in a cool place until needed.
- When working with white fondant, remember everything must be very clean and fluff-free! Whatever is on your hands or the bench will stick to the fondant and show up.

# Rugby Ball and Boots Cupcakes

Any boys playing rugby barefoot on a frosty morning could do with a pair of these!
*Makes 12*

12 vanilla cupcakes (see page 99)

vanilla buttercream (see page 135)

green colour gel

coupler

nozzle for grass

piping bag

fondant: 150 g brown; 150 g black; 50 g white

stitching tool or toothpick

small paintbrush

edible glue (see page 17)

dusting puff

small fondant rolling pin

1. Bake and cool cupcakes as per the recipe.
2. Prepare and colour buttercream by adding green colour gel and mixing thoroughly. If using liquid food colour, watch you don't add too much as it will thin your icing down and may cause it to separate. Fit the nozzle to the end of your piping bag and fill with buttercream. Set aside.
3. To make the rugby ball, take a large marble-sized piece of brown fondant and roll into a ball, then roll the ends to create the ball shape. Using a stitching tool (or toothpick), run this around the top and sides to create the stitching look. Make 11 more rugby balls.
4. To make the boots, roll two small marble-sized balls of black fondant the same size. Roll each ball into a short sausage with slightly rounded ends, place on the bench and gently push the rounded end of a small paintbrush into the top of one end to create the top of the boot.
5. Very thinly roll out white fondant and cut short strips for the detailing on the sides of the boot. Gently press to the side of the boot. If the fondant strips don't stick, brush a very small amount of edible glue to one side of the strip.
6. Continue making boots. You will need two boots per cupcake.
7. To cover the cupcake with grass, hold the piping bag close to but not touching the cupcake and squeeze the buttercream out, ensuring it can attach to the top of the cupcake. Keep squeezing gently as you pull the bag away. When you stop squeezing the icing will stop and the grass will break off. Repeat with all the cupcakes.
8. Gently place the balls on top, then the boots to the front of the ball.

*TIPS*
- Always ensure the fondant is kneaded well before using so that it is soft and pliable. If it isn't, you may end up with creases in your decorations.
- When using edible glue to attach fondant to fondant, ensure you only use a very small amount. Too much will end up dissolving the sugar in the fondant and making your pieces very sticky. When using darker colours you may find that the colour leaches out if too much glue is used.
- You can add further detail to the boots by using a very small round nozzle to pipe laces and a bow.
- If you haven't time to make fondant rugby balls, you could use a scorched almond.
- You can add edible cake glitter over the grass to look like the morning dew or pop some small blossoms on the grass.

# Swimming Pool Cupcakes

One mini swimming pool for everyone!
*Makes 12*

2 packets blue jelly

fondant: 100 g white; 50 g red; 200 g ivory; 50 g yellow ; 50 g brown; 50 g green

dusting puff

small rolling pin

paring knife

small paintbrush

edible glue (see page 17)

black edible food marker

12 small round straight-sided cakes (see pages 114–117 and Tips on page 85)

chocolate buttercream (see page 135)

small spatula

round cutter (the same size as the top of the cake)

chocolate finger biscuits

ribbon

1. Make up both jellies to one quantity of boiling water. Line a shallow baking tin with plastic wrap and pour in the jelly. Refrigerate until set.

2. To make the life ring, roll a small log shape with the white fondant and curl it around to create a circle. Roll out red fondant and cut 4 thin strips to glue around the ring for the detail.

3. To make the swimmer, roll two small balls of ivory fondant into logs. Push up one end to create the foot. Using the paring knife, cut in the toes. Hang the feet over the life ring. Cut a small rectangle of yellow fondant for the shorts and snip out a 'V'. Attach to the legs with a little edible glue. Roll a larger ball of ivory fondant into a teardrop shape for the body. Sit this on top of the ring; the body will cover the join of the legs. Roll out two small logs for the arms; slightly flatten one end for the hands. Use the paring knife to cut in the fingers. Attach to the top of the teardrop to create shoulders. You can place the arms where you want them to go by using a little edible glue. To make the head, roll a ball of ivory fondant and place on the bench. Using the side of your little finger, gently make an impression across the front of the face for the eyes. Use the end of a small paintbrush to make two indentations for the eyes. Roll two small balls of white fondant and pop into the indentations. Add the pupils using an edible food marker. Roll two very small balls of ivory fondant into a teardrop shape and attach to the side of the head for ears. Make one slightly larger teardrop for the nose. For the hair, take a small ball of brown fondant and flatten it out using your fingers. Gently stretch it out to the size and shape needed and attach to the head with a little glue. Draw the tip of the paring knife over the hair to give it some detail. Attach the head to the body using a little glue.

4. Your little fondant swimmer is ready to go into the pool. Repeat to make 12 swimmers.

5. Bake and cool cakes as per the recipe. Prepare the buttercream.

6. Trim the cakes so they will sit flat. Using the spatula, cover each of the cakes with chocolate buttercream.

7. Remove the jelly from the fridge. Using the cutter, cut out 12 rounds of jelly and place on top of the cakes.

8. Push the chocolate finger biscuits into the sides of the cake. Wrap and tie the ribbon around each of the cakes.

9. Place a life ring and swimmer on top of the jelly.

*TIPS*
- You could display these little pool cakes on a cake board and pipe grass around the base of each cake. Little cocktail umbrellas are fun to put around the pool.
- If time is not on your side, you can buy jelly rings and gummy babies in the sweets aisle of the supermarket, and Tiny Teddy biscuits are great to use as well.
- Use concentrated gel colours to darken the colour of the jelly, if necessary.
- You can purchase small, straight-sided cake tins from specialty cake shops or, if making with cupcakes, build the sides straight by turning the cupcake upside-down, removing the paper case and applying a thicker layer of buttercream to the narrow end to straighten up the sides.

# Weta Cupcakes

My boys are not so keen on real creepy critters, but these ones look pretty snazzy on top of a cupcake.
*Makes 12*

12 chocolate cupcakes (see page 90)

chocolate buttercream (see page 135)

black colour gel

small spatula

fondant: 50 g green; 50 g chocolate/brown; 50 g yellow; 50 g pink; 50 g orange

dusting puff

small rolling pin

leaf cutter

thin modelling foam

veining tool

12 small chocolate-covered log-shaped sweets (eg Cadbury Boost or mini chocolate-covered Flake)

small round cutter (approximately 1½ cm)

small paintbrush

edible glue (see page 17)

very small round nozzle and small round nozzle

liquorice string

coupler

piping bag

1. Bake and cool cupcakes as per the recipe. Prepare the buttercream.

2. Take 1 tbsp chocolate buttercream and put into a small dish. Add black colour gel to make black buttercream and set aside.

3. Using the spatula, spread chocolate buttercream over the top of each cupcake.

4. Knead the green fondant until soft and pliable and roll out to 3 mm thick. Dust the work surface if the icing is sticking. Cut out 6 leaves and place on thin modelling foam. Using the veining tool, run a line down the centre of the leaf and then angle veins from the outside edge to the middle. Gently shape the leaves by pinching the base and twisting the top slightly. Evenly space the leaves around the top of the cupcake. Repeat with the other cupcakes.

5. To make the weta, remove the chocolate log sweets from the packaging and set on the work surface. Roll out the brown fondant and, using the small round cutter, cut out three discs and place, overlapping, on the back of each log. Attach with edible glue.

6. To make the head, roll small balls of brown fondant slightly smaller than the end of the log. By flattening the ball slightly it will make the head the same size as the end of the log. Before attaching to the body, use the back of the paintbrush to imprint the eyes and roll the curved edge of the nozzle to create the mouth. Cut two short strips of liquorice for the antennae, push the end of the paintbrush into the top of the head, dip the end of the liquorice into the glue and insert into the hole. Spread a little buttercream onto the back of the head and gently press onto the end of the log. Glue the body onto the top of the cupcake with a little buttercream.

7. Against the body of the weta are the joints for the legs. Roll two very small balls of brown fondant and stack them on top of each other to create the top joint of the leg. Using the end of the paintbrush, make a hole in the centre. Attach to the side of the body. Each weta needs six of these joints (three on each side).

**8** The little shoes are a small ball of coloured fondant rolled into a slight teardrop shape. Place on the work surface and with the end of the paintbrush push a hole into the wide end. Cut 6 short lengths of liquorice for the legs. Press one end into the hole made in the joints and the other into the shoe. Press the shoe down and attach to the buttercream. If the shoe is sitting on a leaf you will need to brush on a little glue to attach it.

**9** The bow on the front of the shoe is made with buttercream and the very small round nozzle. Pipe a figure eight on the front of the shoe, then the ribbon.

**10** Fit the piping bag with the small round nozzle and black buttercream, then pipe the three strips along the weta's back.

**11** Repeat to make 12 wetas.

*TIPS*
- If you have trouble finding liquorice string, you can pull apart the liquorice twists available at the supermarket.
- A tube of readymade and coloured black buttercream (from specialty cake shops) is handy to have for small-detail jobs like this one.
- The wetas can be made ahead of time and stored.

# Cupcake Recipes

The following recipes can be used for making regular-sized cupcakes, as well as mini cupcakes. If making mini cupcakes, the cooking time should be reduced to 8–10 minutes. It is easy to overcook mini cupcakes so test and check regularly.

## Chocolate Cupcakes

*Makes 12*

100 g standard flour
25 g cocoa
140 g caster sugar
1½ tsp baking powder
¼ tsp salt
50 g unsalted butter, at room temperature
120 ml milk
1 egg
¼ tsp vanilla extract

1. Preheat the oven to 170°C (150°C fan-forced). Line a 12-hole muffin pan with paper cases.
2. Sift together flour, cocoa, sugar, baking powder and salt into the bowl of an electric mixer.
3. Add butter and mix on low speed until you get a sandy consistency and everything is well combined.
4. Whisk the milk, egg and vanilla extract together in a bowl. Slowly pour about half into the flour mixture, beat to combine and turn the mixer up to medium-high speed to get rid of any lumps.
5. Turn the mixer down to a slower speed and slowly pour in the remaining milk mixture (scrape any unmixed ingredients from the side of the bowl with a rubber spatula). Continue mixing until the mixture is smooth. Do not over-mix.
6. Spoon the mixture into cupcake cases until two-thirds full and bake in the preheated oven for 15–20 minutes, or until the cupcakes bounce back when lightly touched.
7. Remove the cupcakes from the pan and place on a wire rack to cool completely.

## Chocolate Chilli Cupcakes

This recipe makes an interesting alternative to plain chocolate cupcakes.
*Makes 24*

170 g dark chocolate, chopped
260 g standard flour
1 tsp baking soda
½ tsp cinnamon
2 tsp chilli powder
250 g butter, softened
125 g sugar
125 g brown sugar
4 large eggs, at room temperature
1 cup buttermilk, at room temperature
1 tsp vanilla extract

1. Preheat the oven to 180°C (160°C fan-forced). Line two 12-hole muffin pans with paper cases.
2. To melt the chocolate place chopped chocolate in a heatproof bowl and place over a saucepan of simmering water, stirring occasionally until chocolate is melted and completely smooth. Remove from heat and let cool for 10 minutes or until lukewarm.
3. Sift the flour, baking soda, cinnamon and chilli powder together in a bowl and set aside.
4. Using an electric mixer, cream the butter until smooth. Add the sugars and beat for about 3 minutes or until light and fluffy.
5. Add the eggs one at a time, beating well after each addition.
6. Add the chocolate, mixing until well incorporated.
7. Mix in the dry ingredients, in three stages, alternating with the buttermilk and vanilla. With each addition, mix until ingredients are just incorporated but not over-mixed.
8. Divide the batter between the paper cases.
9. Bake in the preheated oven for 20–25 minutes or until a skewer comes out clean when inserted. Remove the cupcakes from the pan and place on a wire rack to cool completely.

*TIPS*
- If you don't want the cupcakes to have too much spice, reduce the chilli to 1 tsp.
- You can easily halve this recipe to make 12 cupcakes.

# Chocolate Mud Cupcakes
*Makes 12*

1½ tbsp instant coffee
180 ml boiling water
125 g butter, chopped
150 g dark chocolate, finely chopped
2 eggs
2 tbsp vegetable oil
⅓ cup buttermilk
130 g standard flour
1 tsp baking powder
¼ tsp baking soda
1 cup brown sugar
¼ cup cocoa

1. Preheat the oven to 160°C (140°C fan-forced). Line a 12-hole muffin pan with paper cases.
2. In a small bowl, mix the coffee and boiling water together.
3. Put the butter and chocolate into a mixing bowl and pour the hot coffee over it. Stir until the chocolate has melted and the mixture is smooth. Cool.
4. In a separate bowl, whisk together the eggs, oil and buttermilk.
5. Sift the flour, baking powder, baking soda, sugar and cocoa together in a bowl.
6. Make a well in the centre of the dry ingredients, pour in the egg mixture and stir until well combined.
7. Lastly, add the cooled chocolate mixture and stir until thoroughly combined.
8. Spoon the mixture into the paper cases until just above halfway and bake in the preheated oven for approximately 25 minutes or until a skewer comes out clean when inserted.
9. Remove the cupcakes from the pan and place on a wire rack to cool completely before decorating.

*TIPS*
• Add chocolate chips or orange zest to the cake batter to add a little something extra to the cakes.
• Push a piece of chocolate into the uncooked batter, then bake. A sweet treat when you bite into it!

# Carrot Cupcakes

*Makes 12*

180 g standard flour
1 tsp baking powder
½ tsp baking soda
1 tsp cinnamon
200 g caster sugar
2 eggs
100 ml vegetable oil
1 tsp vanilla
2 large carrots, peeled and grated
50 g crushed pineapple, drained
45 g pecans, chopped

1. Preheat the oven to 180°C (160° fan-forced). Line a 12-hole muffin pan with cupcake cases.
2. Sift the flour, baking powder, baking soda and cinnamon together in a bowl and set aside.
3. Beat together the sugar and eggs until thick and pale — approximately 5 minutes.
4. Pour in the oil and add vanilla. Beat until smooth.
5. Remove from the mixer and fold in the flour until just combined. Be careful not to over-mix.
6. Lastly, fold through the grated carrots, crushed pineapple and pecans.
7. Divide the batter evenly between the cupcake cases and bake for 20–25 minutes. Test by inserting a skewer into the top of a cupcake. If it comes out clean, the cupcakes are cooked.
8. Remove from the pan and place on a wire rack to cool completely.

# Honey Cupcakes
*Makes 12*

100 ml cream
175 g honey
1 cup standard flour
½ tsp mixed spice
1 tsp cinnamon
½ tsp baking powder
½ tsp baking soda
½ cup canola oil
½ cup caster sugar
zest of one orange
2 eggs

1. Preheat the oven to 180°C (160° fan-forced). Line a 12-hole muffin pan with paper cases.
2. Heat the cream and honey over low to medium heat until honey is melted and well combined. Be careful not to allow it to boil. Set aside to cool slightly.
3. Sift together in a mixing bowl the flour, mixed spice, cinnamon, baking powder and baking soda.
4. Place the oil, sugar and orange zest into the bowl of a stand mixer and beat until well mixed together.
5. Add eggs, one at a time, beating well between additions.
6. Remove bowl and, using a large spoon or spatula, fold in the flour until just combined. Add the cream mixture and gently fold through. Take care not to over-mix or this will toughen the cupcakes.
7. Spoon evenly into the cupcake cases and bake for 20–25 minutes or until the cupcakes bounce back when lightly touched.
8. Remove the cupcakes from the pan and place on a wire rack to cool completely.

*TIP*
- Try baking these cupcakes using manuka honey. It has a wonderful flavour that really comes through in the end result.

# Lemon Cupcakes

*Makes 12*

225 g standard flour
pinch salt
¾ tsp baking powder
¼ tsp baking soda
150 g unsalted butter, softened
170 g caster sugar
3 eggs
zest and juice of 1 large lemon
½ cup milk, at room temperature

1. Preheat the oven to 180°C (160° fan-forced). Line a 12-hole muffin pan with paper cases.
2. Sift together the flour, salt, baking powder and baking soda and set aside.
3. Cream butter and sugar until light and fluffy. Remember to scrape down the sides of the bowl as you go.
4. Add the eggs, beating well between each addition. Beat in the lemon zest and juice.
5. Gently alternate mixing in the milk and flour mixtures, using a large metal spoon.
6. Spoon the mixture into cupcake cases and bake for 20–25 minutes or until the cupcakes bounce back when lightly touched.
7. Remove the cupcakes from the pan and place on a wire rack to cool completely.

# Peanut Butter Cupcakes

*Makes 12*

125 g unsalted butter, at room temperature
150 g dark brown sugar
1 tsp vanilla
125 g smooth peanut butter
1 egg, lightly beaten
180 g standard flour
1 tsp baking powder
½ cup milk

1. Preheat the oven to 180°C (160°C fan-forced). Line a 12-hole muffin pan with paper cases.
2. Cream butter, sugar and vanilla until light and fluffy, scraping down the sides of the bowl as you go.
3. Add the peanut butter and beat well to combine. Pour in the egg and beat.
4. In a separate bowl, sift together the flour and baking powder. Fold into the butter mixture along with the milk.
5. Divide the batter among the cupcake cases until just above halfway and bake in the preheated oven for approximately 20 minutes or until a skewer comes out clean when inserted.
6. Remove the cupcakes from the pan and place on a wire rack to cool completely.

# Red Velvet Cupcakes

*Makes 24*

325 g standard flour
1 tsp baking powder
½ tsp salt
50 ml red food colouring
2 tbsp cocoa
120 g unsalted butter, softened
1½ cups caster sugar
2 eggs
1 tsp vanilla extract
1 cup buttermilk, at room temperature
1 tsp white vinegar
1 tsp baking soda

1. Preheat the oven to 180°C (160°C fan-forced). Line two 12-hole muffin pans with paper cases.
2. Sift together the flour, baking powder and salt into a bowl and set aside.
3. In a small bowl or jug, mix together the food colouring and cocoa to form a smooth paste.
4. Beat together the butter and sugar until light and fluffy.
5. Add the eggs one at a time, beating well after each addition.
6. Add the vanilla and red cocoa paste. Mix in well, scraping down the sides of the bowl once or twice as you go.
7. Add the flour alternately with the buttermilk, starting and finishing with the flour.
8. Mix together the vinegar and baking soda in a small bowl. Add to the cupcake batter and stir to mix in quickly.
9. Divide the batter between the cupcake cases until just above halfway and bake in the preheated oven for 20–25 minutes or until the tops spring back when lightly touched.
10. Remove the cupcakes from the pans and place on a wire rack to cool completely.

*TIPS*
- This recipe works well as a cake also. Grease and line two 20 cm round sponge tins, divide the mixture between the tins and bake for 40–45 minutes.
- Great as a cake base for cake pops!
- Baking soda is activated and starts working once it come in contact with liquid. It is best cooked straight away.

## Strawberries and Cream Cupcakes

*Makes 12*

225 g standard flour
2 tsp baking powder
100 g unsalted butter, softened
150 g caster sugar
zest of 1 lemon
juice of ½ lemon
2 eggs
⅓ cup cream
120 g white chocolate, finely chopped or grated
1 cup fresh strawberries, roughly chopped, or ½ cup dried strawberries, slightly crushed

1. Preheat the oven to 180°C (160°C fan-forced). Line a 12-hole muffin pan with paper cases.
2. Sift together the flour and baking powder and set aside.
3. Cream butter and sugar until light and fluffy, scraping down the bowl as you go.
4. Add lemon zest and juice and beat in well.
5. Add the eggs one at a time, beating well after each addition.
6. Add the sifted dry ingredients to the creamed mixture alternately with the cream, starting and finishing with the flour.
7. Gently fold through the white chocolate and strawberries.
8. Divide the batter between the cupcake cases until just above halfway and bake in the preheated oven for 20–25 minutes or until the tops spring back when lightly touched or a skewer comes out clean when inserted.
9. Remove the cupcakes from the pan and place on a wire rack to cool completely.

*TIP*
- Although fresh strawberries are not available all year, you can make these gorgeous cupcakes using dried strawberries.

# Vanilla Cupcakes

*Makes 12*

150 g unsalted butter, softened
150 g caster sugar
1 tsp vanilla bean paste or 2 tsp vanilla extract
175 g standard flour
1 tsp baking powder
pinch salt
3 eggs, lightly beaten

1. Preheat the oven to 180°C (160°C fan-forced). Line a 12-hole muffin pan with paper cases.
2. Cream butter and sugar until light and fluffy, scraping down the bowl a couple of times as you go.
3. Add vanilla paste or extract and beat until well blended.
4. Sift together the flour, baking powder and salt into a bowl.
5. Pour the egg in three lots into the creamed mixture, beating well after each addition.
6. Reduce the speed on the mixer to slow and gradually add the sifted dry ingredients, being careful not to over-mix.
7. Divide the batter between the cupcake cases until just above halfway and bake in the preheated oven for 20–25 minutes or until the tops spring back when lightly touched.
8. Remove from the pan and place on a wire rack to cool completely.

*TIP*
- To add colour to the vanilla cupcake batter, it is best to use a concentrated gel colour (available from specialty cake shops). You won't need a lot and, because it is a gel, it won't alter the consistency of the batter. The colour will bake out slightly on cooking so colour the batter a couple of shades darker. Add the colour half a teaspoon at a time and mix well.

# Kiwiana Cake Pops

# How to Make Cake Pops

1 x 20 cm cake (see pages 114–117), to make approximately 24 cake balls

chocolate chips, chopped dried fruit, etc. (optional)

½ cup buttercream, chocolate ganache or cream cheese icing (see pages 131 and 135–136)

500 g melted chocolate (see page 19)

1. Break the cake into a food processer and, using the metal cutting blade, process until the cake is a crumb consistency.

2. Tip crumbs into a large bowl. Add any chocolate chips, dried fruit, etc., if you wish.

3. Add the buttercream or ganache or cream cheese icing. Mix all together until well combined.

4. Before rolling the cake balls, dampen your hands so the cake doesn't stick to them. Roll cake into 24 balls.

5. Place the cake balls on a tray lined with baking paper and put in the fridge to harden for at least 30 minutes.

6. Melt the chocolate (see page 19) and dip the cake balls into the chocolate.

7. You can freeze the cake balls if you need to make them ahead of time. Defrost them in the fridge before dipping into the chocolate. If the cake balls are dipped while frozen, the chocolate may crack as the cake ball defrosts.

8. You can make cake pops any size and shape. If you are making pops for very young children, make them small. The cake pop sticks can be cut in half so little hands can manage them.

9. If you need to mould the cake balls into a particular shape, do so before putting in the fridge to harden.

# Hokey Pokey Cake Pops

Hokey pokey ice creams are a must on a hot summer's day, but these little cake pops can be enjoyed all year round.
*Makes 24*

1 x 20 cm hokey pokey cake (see page 115)

½ cup hokey pokey, chopped (see page 122)

1 cup caramel buttercream (see page 130)

24 mini ice cream cones (available from specialty food stores)

350 g white chocolate, roughly chopped

hokey pokey sprinkles

1. Line a baking tray with baking paper.

2. Break the cake into a food processer and, using the metal cutting blade, process until the cake is a crumb consistency.

3. Place crumbs in a mixing bowl and add chopped hokey pokey. Mix together with the buttercream.

4. Using damp hands, roll the mixture into balls large enough to fit on top of the mini cones. Put cake balls on prepared tray. Place in the fridge for 30 minutes to harden.

5. Place the white chocolate in a heatproof bowl and place over a saucepan of simmering water to melt (see page 19). Stir chocolate while it is melting.

6. When the chocolate is melted and smooth, turn the heat off but leave the bowl on top of the saucepan to keep warm.

7. Remove the cake balls from the fridge. Dip the base of each ball in the melted chocolate and place chocolate side-down onto the mini cone. The melted chocolate will act as glue, fixing the cake ball to the top of the cone. Stand the mini cones in a shallow ramekin to dry.

8. Once dry, take each mini cone and dip the cake end into the melted chocolate to coat the ball. Let excess chocolate run off before turning upright and sprinkling with the hokey pokey sprinkles.

*TIP*

- If you wish to use chocolate cake for the cake ball, you may need to dip the cake ball twice into the melted chocolate so the dark colour doesn't show through.

# Ice Cream Sundae Cake Pops

With a lovely big Jaffa on the top, these cake pops are true Kiwiana.
*Makes 12*

1 x 24 cm rich chocolate cake (see page 114)

½ cup chocolate chips or chopped dried fruit, or chopped nuts

1 cup chocolate ganache (see page 131)

12 dark chocolate cups (available from specialty food stores)

350 g white chocolate, roughly chopped

100 g dark chocolate, melted (see page 19)

100s and 1000s

12 Jaffas or fresh cherries

12 candy sticks

1. Line a baking tray with baking paper.
2. Break the cake into a food processor and, using the metal cutting blade, process until the cake is a crumb consistency.
3. Place crumbs in a mixing bowl, add chocolate chips or chopped fruit or nuts and mix in chocolate ganache.
4. Using damp hands, roll the mixture into balls large enough to fill the inside of a chocolate cup. Place cake balls on the prepared baking tray and refrigerate for 30 minutes.
5. Once the balls are hardened, melt the white chocolate in a heatproof bowl over a saucepan of simmering water (see page 19).
6. When the chocolate is melted and smooth, turn the heat off but leave the bowl on top of the saucepan to keep warm.
7. Remove the cake balls from the fridge and dip the base of one ball in the melted white chocolate. Sit the ball chocolate side-down in the chocolate cup. The melted chocolate will act like glue, fixing the cake ball to the chocolate cup. Repeat with the remaining cake balls and cups.
8. Once the chocolate has set, take a cup and turn upside-down to coat the cake ball with chocolate. Roll in the melted chocolate to ensure the white chocolate comes right down to the top of the cup. Let the excess drip off before turning right side up.
9. When the white chocolate has hardened, pour 1 tsp of melted dark chocolate onto the top of the cake pop and gently massage out until it starts to run down the sides. Sprinkle with 100s and 1000s, pop a Jaffa on top and gently push a candy stick into the side before the chocolate sets too hard.
10. Repeat with the remaining chocolate cups.

# Jaffa Cake Pops

These are super-quick to make, and can be adapted for many other flavours.
*Makes 24*

250 g dark chocolate, chopped

½ cup cream

1 x 24 cm rich chocolate cake (see page 114)

½ cup chocolate chips (optional)

500 g white chocolate, roughly chopped

red food colouring (oil-based or powder)

2 drops orange oil or 1 tsp orange essence

24 cake pop sticks

polystyrene block (to stand pops in while drying)

red sugar (see Tips on page 109)

1. Place the dark chocolate in a bowl. Bring the cream to the boil and pour over the chocolate. Allow to stand for a couple of minutes before using a whisk to gently stir until smooth.

2. Break the cake into a food processor and, using the metal cutting blade, process until the cake is a crumb consistency.

3. Place crumbs in a mixing bowl and add chocolate chips, if using. Pour half the chocolate mixture into the cake crumbs and mix until well combined. Add more chocolate, if needed.

4. Line a baking tray with baking paper.

5. Using damp hands, roll the mixture into balls and place on the prepared tray. Once all the balls have been rolled, refrigerate for at least 30 minutes to allow the cake balls to harden.

6. Put the white chocolate in a heatproof bowl and place over a saucepan of simmering water, ensuring the bottom of the bowl does not touch the top of the simmering water. Gently stir as the chocolate melts. Add the red food colouring a little at a time until the desired shade is achieved.

7. Add the orange oil or essence to the red chocolate to flavour. The oils are a concentrate so taste the chocolate as you go to avoid the flavour getting too strong.

8. Remove the cake balls from the fridge once the red chocolate is ready.

9. Dip the end of a cake pop stick into the melted chocolate and push into the end of a cake ball. The chocolate will act as a glue to help prevent your cake pop becoming a cake 'plop' when you dip it entirely in the chocolate. Push the stick into the polystyrene block and allow to dry. Repeat with all the cake balls.

10. Once dry, dip and roll the cake pops in the chocolate to completely cover the ball with chocolate. Gently turn the stick, allowing the excess chocolate to drip off.

11. Hold the cake pop over the bowl of coloured sugar and sprinkle the sugar all over to coat the entire cake pop. Place back into the polystyrene to dry. Continue with the remaining cake pops.

TIPS
- To make spearmint-flavoured cake pops, change the flavouring to spearmint oil and colour the white chocolate spearmint green.
- When colouring/flavouring chocolate, always use oil-based or powder colouring. Water-based colouring/flavouring will cause the chocolate to seize and render it useless. If the chocolate seizes, it will look grainy or form a hard lump. This is caused by moisture getting into the chocolate.
- To colour sugar, put 1 cup sugar into a plastic bag and add a little red colour gel. Seal the top of the bag and massage until the colour is evenly blended with the sugar, adding more colour if you feel it needs it. It is a good idea to use a concentrated colour gel as opposed to liquid colour as it won't dissolve the sugar.

# Sheep Pops in a Paddock

When I was young I used to stay at my cousin's farm where there would be motherless lambs in a playpen by the Aga in the kitchen during lambing season. I never got tired of their bleating!
*Makes 24*

1 x 24 cm rich chocolate cake (see page 114)

chocolate buttercream (see page 135)

25 cm cake board

fondant: 1 kg green; 50 g brown; 20 g yellow; 20 g white; 20 g pink; 50 g black

dusting puff

rolling pin

cooled boiled water

paring knife

20 cm polystyrene cake dummy

cake turntable

dowelling (with a point sharpened at one end)

100 g green royal icing (see recipe page 137 and colouring instructions on page 14)

edible glue (see page 17)

small blossom plunger cutter

nozzle for grass

coupler

piping bag

small paintbrush

edible glitter

black edible food marker

*(continued on next page)*

1. Line a baking tray with baking paper.

2. Break the cake into a food processor and, using the metal cutting blade, process until the cake is a crumb consistency.

3. Place crumbs in a mixing bowl and mix in the chocolate buttercream.

4. Using damp hands, roll the mixture into balls large enough to be the sheep's bodies (approximately 30 g each). Place on the prepared tray and put into the fridge to harden.

5. To cover the cake board, knead 500 g green fondant until it is soft and pliable. Dust the work surface lightly with the dusting puff. Roll out the fondant in a circle until it is approximately 5 mm thick, turning the fondant as you are rolling to ensure it doesn't stick to the work surface.

6. Hold the cake board over the top of the rolled out fondant to gauge if it is large enough. Brush the top of the board lightly with cooled boiled water. Using your rolling pin, move the rolled fondant and place on top of the board. Smooth the icing down with the palm of your hand. Trim excess icing from around the edge using a paring knife.

7. To cover the cake dummy with fondant, add the trimmings from covering the board to the remaining green fondant and knead together until soft and pliable. Roll icing out to approximately 5 mm thick. Brush the cake dummy with cooled boiled water and shake off the excess moisture. Place the cake dummy onto a turntable. Using the rolling pin to move the fondant, place fondant over the dummy. Working quickly, smooth the top using the palm of your hand. Gently push the icing into the sides, turning the dummy as you gently move around and down. Always push the icing into the dummy sides and be careful not to stretch the icing downward, which puts stress on the top edge and may causing cracking and tearing. When the icing is attached and smooth on the cake dummy, trim around the bottom.

8. Use the sharp end of the dowelling to gently push enough holes into the top for the cake pop sticks. Twist the dowel out of the dummy; this will prevent the fondant from lifting.

9. Spread a little royal icing onto the middle of the cake board and place the cake dummy centred on top. The royal icing will fix the cake to the board. Place the cake board onto the turntable to decorate.

white nonpareils

350 g white chocolate, roughly chopped

12 cake pop sticks

polystyrene block (to stand pops in while drying)

1 m brown ribbon

double-sided tape

10. To make the fence, knead the brown fondant until soft and pliable. Roll out to 5 mm thick. Cut strips to the desired length and width for the fence posts. Cut a rough point at the top of each one. Run the point of the paring knife along the post to create a wood look. Brush a small amount of edible glue on the back of each post and fix to the side of the cake dummy. Repeat with the remaining posts. The railings are done in the same manner; they are cut thinner and a little longer. Attach the rails to the cake dummy.

11. Roll out the white fondant and, using the small blossom cutter, cut out blossoms. Repeat with the pink fondant. Roll a small amount of yellow fondant and push into the centre of each blossom. Set aside.

12. Attach the nozzle for grass to the coupler and fill the piping bag with a little green royal icing. Pipe grass around the holes on the top and place blossoms in the grass.

13. Pipe grass around the base of the cake and again place the blossoms around.

14. Using a dry paintbrush, brush a little edible glitter over the top of the cake in between the grassed holes.

15. To make the sheep heads and legs, take a ball of black fondant about the size of a pea. Roll it slightly thinner at one end and flatten to create the head. Roll two small balls of black into a teardrop shape and flatten for the ears. Roll a small ball of pink into a teardrop shape and flatten, attach this to the black ear. Repeat for the remaining ears. Attach ears to the top of the head with a little edible glue, the pink side underneath. Roll two very small balls of white for the eyes and attach to the head. Using the edible food marker, dot the pupil onto the eyes. Set aside to dry.

16. For the legs, roll small amounts of black fondant into a short log shape. Push the back of a knife into one end to create the hoof. Repeat for the remaining legs. Set aside to dry.

17. Place the white nonpareils in a bowl.

18. Melt the white chocolate in a heatproof bowl over the top of a saucepan of simmering water, making sure the bottom of the bowl doesn't touch the top of the water.

**19** Take the cake balls out of the fridge, dip a cake pop stick into the melted chocolate and push it approximately three-quarters of the way into a cake ball. The melted chocolate on the stick will act as glue so the cake ball won't fall off the stick when dipped into the melted chocolate. Push the stick into the polystyrene block and allow to dry. Repeat with the remaining cake balls.

**20** Once dry, dip each cake pop into the melted white chocolate and roll to ensure the ball is completely coated. Tap off excess chocolate before holding over the bowl of nonpareils and sprinkling all over to cover. Push into the polystyrene block to dry. Repeat with remaining cake pops.

**21** Attach the heads and legs to the cake balls by putting a little of the melted chocolate onto the back of the head and the top end of the legs. Press firmly but gently onto the cake pop and hold until the chocolate sets. As each sheep is completed, push the stick into the holes on the top of the fondant-covered cake dummy. Repeat with the remaining cake pops to complete your paddock full of sheep.

**22** Lastly, attach the ribbon around the edge of the cake board using the double-sided tape.

*TIPS*
- You could replace the cake dummy with a real 20 cm cake if you need to cater for more people.
- If all your cake pops don't fit into the paddock, fill tall glasses with candy-coated chocolate and stand the sticks in the glasses. They look really effective on the table.

# Cake Pop Cake Recipes

## Rich Chocolate Cake

Chocolate cake is a favourite of many. This is a super-rich cake that keeps well.
*Makes one 24 cm round cake*

½ cup vegetable oil
250 g dark chocolate, roughly chopped
1 cup strong hot coffee
260 g standard flour
2 tsp baking soda
1 tsp baking powder
200 g caster sugar
½ cup Dutch process cocoa
2 large eggs
1 cup buttermilk, at room temperature

1. Preheat the oven to 180°C (160°C fan-forced). Grease and line a 24 cm round cake tin.
2. Place oil and chocolate into a mixing bowl and pour over the hot coffee. Using a whisk, stir until the chocolate is melted and the mixture is smooth. Set aside to cool.
3. In a large bowl, sift together the flour, baking soda, baking powder, sugar and cocoa.
4. Add the eggs to the cooled chocolate mixture. Mix well.
5. Add the chocolate mixture to the dry ingredients alternately with the buttermilk. Whisk to combine thoroughly.
6. Pour into prepared tin and bake in the preheated oven for approximately 1 hour. Fudgy crumbs should still adhere to a skewer when tested.
7. Cool for 15 minutes in the tin before turning out onto a wire rack to cool completely.

*TIPS*
- The coffee helps to bring out the chocolate flavour while reducing some of the sweetness.
- To make a jaffa-flavoured cake, add ½ tsp orange oil or essence and the zest of 1 orange to the recipe.
- To make a spearmint-flavoured cake, add 1 tsp spearmint essence to the recipe.

# Hokey Pokey Cake

*Makes one 20 cm round cake*

225 g butter
225 g brown sugar
1 tbsp golden syrup
1 tsp vanilla
4 large eggs
225 g standard flour
2 tsp baking powder

1. Preheat the oven to 180°C (160°C fan-forced). Grease and line a 20 cm round cake tin.
2. Cream butter, sugar, golden syrup and vanilla together until light and fluffy.
3. Add the eggs one at a time, beating well after each addition.
4. Sift flour and baking powder together.
5. Add to butter mixture and mix gently until just combined.
6. Spoon into the prepared tin and bake in the preheated oven for 45 minutes or until a skewer comes out clean when inserted.
7. Leave in the tin for 10 minutes before turning out onto a wire rack to cool completely.

*TIP*
- This recipe will also make 18 standard sized cupcakes. Divide the cake batter between the cupcake cases and bake at the above temperature for 10–15 minutes, or until the top of the cupcake springs back when lightly touched.

# Vanilla Bean Cake

*Makes one 24 cm round cake*

225 g unsalted butter, softened
275 caster sugar
1 tsp vanilla bean paste or 1 vanilla bean, split and seeds scraped
3 eggs
295 g standard flour
1 tbsp baking powder
¼ tsp salt
1¾ cups milk

1. Preheat the oven to 180°C (160°C fan-forced). Grease and line a 24 cm round cake tin.
2. Cream butter and sugar until light and fluffy. Add vanilla bean paste or vanilla seeds from pod.
3. Add the eggs one at a time, beating well after each addition.
4. In another bowl, sift dry ingredients together.
5. Add dry ingredients to the creamed mixture alternately with the milk.
6. Mix until just combined but not over-mixed.
7. Pour into prepared tin and bake in the preheated oven for 40 minutes or until a skewer comes out clean when inserted into the cake.
8. Leave in tin for 10 minutes before turning out onto a wire rack to cool completely.

# Rich Fruit Cake

*Makes one 23 cm square cake*

225 g butter, softened
225 g brown sugar
1 tsp each vanilla, lemon and almond essence
1 tsp each ground ginger and cinnamon
½ tsp each ground nutmeg and ground cloves
6 eggs
350 g high grade flour
1½ kg mixed dried fruit
zest and juice of 1 orange

1. Preheat the oven to 140°C (120°C fan-forced). Grease and line a 23 cm square cake tin with several layers of baking paper.
2. Cream butter and sugar until light and fluffy.
3. Beat in the essence and spices. Add a tablespoon or two of the measured flour to prevent the butter from splitting.
4. Add the eggs one at a time, beating well after each addition.
5. Place the dried fruit into a bowl. Mix the remaining flour into the fruit and coat well.
6. Using a wooden spoon, stir the fruit into the creamed butter mixture.
7. Add orange zest and juice. Mix together well.
8. Spoon into the prepared tin and smooth the top. Bake in the preheated oven for 3-4 hours or until a skewer comes out clean when inserted.
9. Remove cake from the oven and leave in tin to cool completely before turning out onto a wire rack.

*TIPS*
- To add to the cake's richness, soak the fruit in brandy or cold tea for a couple of days before making the cake.
- Coating the fruit with flour will prevent the fruit from sinking to the bottom of the cake.
- If you are planning on making the mini present cakes to give as a gift, the fruit cake can be made well ahead of time and left to mature.

# Whoopie Pies

## What is a Whoopie Pie?

Whoopie pie — is it a cake or a biscuit? The whoopie pie is certainly taking its place on the tables of many celebrations these days.

It is unclear where the whoopie pie originated, but many people believe it was from Pennsylvanian Amish women who used leftover cake batter to bake small cakes, then sandwiched them together with a creamy marshmallow filling. The pies would make great sweet treats for their husbands going out into the fields to work and it is believed they would call out 'Whoopie!' when they discovered one in their lunch pail.

Traditionally, the whoopie pie is chocolate with a creamy filling, although many flavours are available now. I have put together a collection of 'Kiwiana' flavours that I hope you will try and enjoy.

# Chocolate Jaffa or Spearmint Whoopie Pies

*Makes approximately 24*

250 g standard flour

pinch salt

75 g cocoa

1½ tsp baking soda

½ tsp baking powder

125 g unsalted butter, at room temperature

200 g dark brown sugar

1 large egg

1 cup buttermilk, at room temperature

1 tsp pure vanilla extract or ½ tsp vanilla bean paste

orange or spearmint chocolate ganache (see page 131)

350 g white chocolate, roughly chopped

orange or spearmint oil, to flavour the chocolate

red or spearmint green oil-based or powder colour

1. Preheat the oven to 200°C (180°C fan-forced). Line two baking trays with baking paper or grease two small whoopie pie tins.

2. In a bowl, sift together flour, salt, cocoa, baking soda and baking powder. Set aside.

3. In the bowl of an electric mixer fitted with the paddle attachment, cream butter and sugar until light and fluffy.

4. Add egg, buttermilk and vanilla. Beat until well combined. Slowly add dry ingredients. Mix until just combined.

5. Using a small ice cream scoop or dessertspoon, place scoops of mixture onto prepared baking trays, leaving a gap between each, or spoon mixture into whoopie pie tins.

6. Bake in the preheated oven for approximately 12 minutes or until dry to the touch. Remove to a wire rack to cool completely. Repeat with remaining batter.

7. Once cooled, spread ganache onto half the whoopie pies. Sandwich together with remaining cakes.

8. To melt, flavour and colour the white chocolate, place the chocolate in a heatproof bowl and put it on top of a saucepan of simmering water. Ensure the bottom of the bowl doesn't touch the top of the simmering water. Stir as the chocolate melts. When the chocolate has melted, add a couple of drops of flavoured oil. Check the taste before adding more. The oils are a concentrate so you won't need much. Add the colouring in the same way, a little at a time, until the desired colour is reached.

9. Dip half of each whoopie pie in the melted chocolate. Allow the excess to drip off before putting onto baking trays lined with baking paper to dry.

# Hokey Pokey Whoopie Pies

*Makes approximately 24*

250 g standard flour

1½ tsp baking powder

120 g butter, or
   60 g butter and 60 g vegetable shortening (e.g. Kremelta), at room temperature

120 g dark brown sugar

1 tsp vanilla essence

2 eggs

½ cup buttermilk, at room temperature

2 tbsp milk

1 tsp baking soda

1 tsp white vinegar

½ cup crushed hokey pokey (see below) or 1 Crunchie bar, roughly chopped

caramel buttercream (see page 130)

1. Preheat the oven to 170°C (150°C fan-forced). Grease or line two baking trays with baking paper or grease two small whoopie pie tins.
2. Sift together the flour and baking powder in a bowl.
3. In the bowl of an electric mixer fitted with the paddle attachment, beat the butter (or butter and shortening) until light in colour.
4. Add the sugar slowly. Beat on medium speed until light and fluffy, scraping down the sides of the bowl. Add vanilla essence.
5. Add the eggs one at a time, beating well for a minute or so after each addition.
6. Add the flour alternately with the buttermilk to the creamed mixture. Mix until just blended. Be careful not to over-mix.
7. In a small bowl, mix together the milk, baking soda and vinegar. Add this and the hokey pokey pieces to the batter and gently mix.
8. Using a small ice cream scoop, place scoops of the mixture on the prepared baking trays or spoon mixture into whoopie pie tins.
9. Bake in the preheated oven for approximately 10–12 minutes or until dry to the touch. Remove to a wire rack to cool completely. Repeat with remaining batter.
10. Spread buttercream onto half the whoopie pies. Sandwich together with remaining cakes. Roll filled whoopie pies in the chopped hokey pokey, or leave plain.

## Hokey Pokey

75 g white sugar

2 tbsp golden syrup

1 tsp baking soda

1. Grease or line a 20 x 30 cm Swiss roll tin with baking paper.
2. Place sugar and golden syrup in a medium saucepan. Heat gently, stirring until the sugar dissolves.
3. Increase the heat and bring to the boil. Boil for 2 minutes. Stir occasionally, if necessary, to prevent burning.
4. Remove from heat. Add baking soda. Stir quickly until mixture froths up rapidly!
5. Pour into prepared tin immediately. Leave until cold and hard, then break into pieces.

*Special thanks to Edmonds Cookery Book for this recipe.*

### TIPS
- Remember to give the carton of buttermilk a good shake before measuring out the required amount.
- Using dark brown sugar adds to the rich caramel flavour, but brown sugar will work also.

# Lamington Whoopie Pies

*Makes approximately 24*

125 g butter, at room temperature

100 g caster sugar

100 g brown sugar

2 eggs

2 tsp vanilla extract or 1 tsp vanilla paste

120 ml buttermilk, at room temperature

300 g standard flour

½ tsp salt

1½ tsp baking powder

2 tbsp milk

1 tsp white wine vinegar

1 tsp baking soda

chocolate icing (see page 126), to coat

½ cup raspberry icing (see page 126), to coat

desiccated coconut, for dredging

whipped cream and raspberry jam, to serve

1. Preheat the oven to 200°C (180°C fan-forced). Line two trays with baking paper or grease two small whoopie pie tins.

2. Cream the butter and sugars until smooth and creamy. Add the eggs and beat well.

3. In a small bowl, mix the vanilla into the buttermilk. Add this mixture to the creamed butter mixture and beat well until combined.

4. Sift together the flour, salt and baking powder. Add half of this to the butter mixture and beat well.

5. Mix together the milk, vinegar and baking soda and add this to the butter mixture. Beat to combine.

6. Add the rest of the flour mixture and beat well to combine.

7. Using a teaspoon or a small ice cream scoop, place scoops of the mixture on the prepared trays, leaving a gap between each, or spoon mixture into the whoopie pie tins.

8. Bake in the preheated oven for 8–10 minutes or until they are just beginning to brown.

9. Remove from the trays or pie tins to a wire rack to cool completely.

10. Using two forks, dip half the cakes into the warm chocolate icing to evenly coat. Allow any excess coating to drip off. Roll the cakes in the coconut to evenly coat, then place on a wire rack. Leave the cakes for approximately 1 hour before sandwiching together with whipped cream.

11. Dip the other half of the cakes into the warm raspberry icing to evenly coat. Allow any excess coating to drip off, then roll in the coconut to evenly coat. Leave for 1 hour before sandwiching together with raspberry jam and whipped cream.

## Chocolate Icing

2 cups icing sugar

⅓ cup cocoa powder

¼ cup milk

¼ cup boiling water

Sift the icing sugar and cocoa together in a medium bowl. Add the milk and water and stir until smooth.

## Raspberry Icing

1 packet raspberry jelly crystals

1 cup boiling water

Dissolve the jelly in the boiling water. Leave until cooled and the mixture has thickened slightly.

*TIP*

- As an alternative, instead of sandwiching individual lamington whoopie pies together, you can serve them with jam and cream on the side as in the photograph opposite.

# Vanilla Whoopie Pies

*Makes approximately 24*

125 g unsalted butter, at room temperature

75 g caster sugar

2 eggs

1½ tsp vanilla extract or 1 tsp vanilla paste

250 g standard flour

pinch salt

1½ tsp baking powder

¾ cup buttermilk, at room temperature

1. Preheat the oven to 190°C (170°C fan-forced). Line two baking trays with baking paper or grease two small whoopie pie tins.
2. In a large mixing bowl, cream together the butter and sugar until light and fluffy.
3. Add the eggs one at a time, beating until well combined between each addition.
4. Add vanilla extract or paste, and beat to combine.
5. Sift together the flour, salt and baking powder into a bowl.
6. Add the flour mixture to the butter mixture alternately with the buttermilk, beginning and ending with the dry ingredients. Mix until just combined.
7. Using an ice cream scoop, place scoops of mixture on the prepared baking trays, leaving a gap between each, or spoon mixture into whoopie pie tins.
8. Bake in the preheated oven for 10–12 minutes or until the tops are springy and just barely dry (the time will depend on the size). Watch carefully to keep from browning.
9. Cool on the tray for 5 minutes before transferring to a wire rack to cool completely.
10. To finish whoopie pies, spread one cake with buttercream or chosen filling and top with another half.

# Fillings for Whoopie Pies

These are the fillings I used but you can sandwich whoopie pies together with any of the icings on pages 135–136.

## Caramel Buttercream

100 g unsalted butter
125 g brown sugar
75 g golden syrup
125 ml cream
1 kg icing sugar, sifted

1. Put the unsalted butter, brown sugar, golden syrup and cream in a small heavy-based saucepan. Stir gently together over medium-low heat until the butter is melted, the mixture is well combined and the sugar has dissolved.
2. Turn the heat up to medium-high and, without stirring, boil for approximately 5 minutes.
3. Take off the heat and allow to cool to room temperature.
4. Pour the mixture into the bowl of an electric mixer. Add half of the icing sugar and, using the flat beater attachment, beat until the mixture is light and fluffy.
5. Add the remaining icing sugar gradually and beat until a spreadable consistency is achieved.
6. If you feel the mixture is a bit too dry, add a little more cream.

*TIP*
- The salt in salted butter cuts through the sweetness of the caramel buttercream filling and enhances the butter flavour. By using unsalted butter you get a sweeter, more caramel-like flavour.

## Chocolate Ganache

250 ml cream
375 g dark or milk chocolate, chopped

1. Bring the cream to the boil and pour over the chopped chocolate.
2. Let stand for a couple of minutes to allow the chocolate to start melting before using a whisk to gently blend the melting chocolate and cream together until smooth.
3. Allow to stand until cooled to room temperature.

*TIPS*
- If you are making chocolate ganache for the tops of cupcakes, add 25 g butter to the cream when bringing to the boil. The addition of butter adds a gloss to the ganache.
- If you are making white chocolate ganache, the chocolate quantity is higher to allow for the higher milk content in the chocolate. Add 125 ml cream to 300 g white chocolate.
- Beat cooled ganache with an electric beater to make it light and fluffy. Beating it will make the ganache more like a buttercream.
- You can flavour the ganache with orange or spearmint oil to fill the jaffa or spearmint whoopie pies. These oils are a concentrate and you will only need to use a couple of drops. Flavoured oils can be found at specialty food stores.
- If making cake pops, the ganache can be used warm to bind the cake crumb together.

# Icings

# Fondant

1 tbsp gelatine
50 ml cold water
1 tbsp glycerine
120 ml liquid glucose
1 kg icing sugar, sifted

1. Sprinkle the gelatine over the cold water and gently heat to dissolve the gelatine crystals. This can be done in the microwave on low heat or by sitting the bowl over a saucepan of simmering water. Be careful not to boil.
2. Once the gelatine has dissolved, remove from heat and add the glycerine and glucose and stir until well combined.
3. Place the icing sugar in a large bowl and pour in the liquid mixture. Mix thoroughly until well combined and smooth, and there are no cracks.
4. Work in a little more icing sugar if the fondant is too sticky. Wrap the fondant tightly in plastic wrap to prevent it drying out.

*TIPS*
- Although fondant is very easy to make and colour, some colours are easier to buy from specialty cake supply shops. Red and black are two colours I always buy, as they both take so much colour to create.
- If you have little helpers in the kitchen when you are decorating your cake, give them a little ball of fondant and some alphabet cutters. Get them to spell out words. They will have so much fun and you will be free to work on your cake without 'assistance'!

## Vanilla Buttercream

200 g unsalted butter, at room temperature
2 tsp vanilla extract
400 g sifted icing sugar
3–4 tbsp cream or milk

1. In the bowl of an electric mixer, cream butter until light and fluffy. Add the vanilla.
2. With mixer on low speed gradually add the icing sugar. Scrape down the side of the bowl.
3. Add the cream or milk and beat on medium-high speed until buttercream is light and fluffy (about 3–4 minutes). Add a little more cream or milk if too dry.

## Chocolate Buttercream

Add ¼ cup cocoa to the above recipe. You will need to add a little extra cream or milk.

## Lemon Buttercream

Reduce vanilla to 1 tsp and the cream or milk to 2 tbsp, add the zest and juice of 1 lemon.

## Peanut Butter Buttercream

200 g unsalted butter, at room temperature
400 g icing sugar, sifted
3–4 tbsp milk or cream
½ cup smooth peanut butter

1. Cream butter until light and fluffy.
2. Gradually add half the icing sugar, beating well to combine. Mix in the milk or cream and then the remaining icing sugar. Continue to beat until the icing is smooth.
3. Lastly, mix in the smooth peanut butter.

*TIP*
• If you make the buttercream ahead of time, beat it again before using to ensure it is soft and fluffy.

## White Buttercream

1 cup vegetable shortening (e.g. Kremelta)
1 tsp vanilla extract
500 g icing sugar, sifted
4–6 tbsp lukewarm water or milk

1. Cream the shortening and vanilla together in a food processor or an electric mixer.
2. Add icing sugar, and with the processor or mixer running, add water or milk 1 tbsp at a time until the required consistency is reached. You will need more liquid in the cooler months and less in the warmer.

*TIPS*
• Using milk helps to cut the sweetness of the icing.
• This icing is a gluten-, egg- and dairy-free option.

## Cream Cheese Icing

50 g unsalted butter, at room temperature
½ tsp vanilla extract
180 g cream cheese, at room temperature
250 g icing sugar, sifted

1. Cream butter and vanilla until smooth and there are no lumps.
2. Add cream cheese and mix to combine.
3. Gradually add the sifted icing sugar and mix until well combined.

## Lemon Cream Cheese Icing

Follow the recipe above and add the zest of 1 lemon and 2 tbsp lemon juice.

## Royal Icing I

2 egg whites
¼ tsp lemon juice
500 g icing sugar, sifted

1. Place the egg whites and lemon juice in the mixing bowl of an electric mixer.
2. With the flat paddle attached, break up the egg whites on low speed.
3. Add sufficient icing sugar and mix well to form the consistency of pouring cream.
4. Continue mixing and adding small quantities of sugar until the desired consistency is reached. Mix for 7–10 minutes. The icing will look like meringue.
5. Allow the icing to rest before using. Cover icing with plastic wrap and a damp cloth.
6. Stir the icing well before using to disperse the air bubbles. Adjust the consistency by adding a little water if needed.

## Royal Icing II

500 g icing sugar
3 tbsp meringue powder
5–6 tbsp lukewarm water

1. Place icing sugar and meringue powder into the bowl of an electric mixer.
2. Using the flat paddle, turn on to low to combine. Add water and mix for 7–10 minutes on medium-low.
3. Add a little more water if the consistency is too stiff.
4. Allow the icing to rest before using. Cover the icing with plastic wrap and a damp cloth.

## Sugar Syrup

1 cup sugar
1 cup water

1. Put the sugar and water into a small saucepan or a heatproof jug. Bring to the boil slowly and boil until all the sugar is dissolved.
2. Flavour the syrup with citrus juice and/or zest, flavoured oils or essence, liqueurs, etc.
3. Store the syrup in a bottle in the fridge.

## Italian Meringue Icing

225 g sugar
80 ml water
2 egg whites

1. Place the sugar and water into a heavy-based saucepan and place over medium heat until the sugar dissolves, stirring occasionally.
2. Bring to a boil and boil until the temperature on a candy thermometer reaches 116°C, approximately 5 minutes. Remove from the heat and let the bubbles subside.
3. In the bowl of an electric mixer, whisk the egg whites to soft peaks.
4. With the mixer on low speed, gradually add the sugar syrup in a thin stream to the egg whites. Turn the mixer speed to high and continue to whisk until the mixture has thickened and cooled — approximately 10 minutes.

*TIP*
• This frosting is best made and eaten on the day. It is delicious and light!

# Conversion Tables

### International measures

Although measuring spoons and cups may vary from New Zealand to Australia and also from Europe to North America, the difference does not generally significantly affect a recipe. Spoon and cup measurements should be level.

1 cup in New Zealand holds 250 ml (8 fl oz)
1 teaspoon holds 5 ml
1 tablespoon holds 15 ml (as in North America and the UK, although an Australian tablespoon holds 20 ml)

### Liquids

| Cup | Metric | Imperial |
|---|---|---|
| ⅛ cup | 30 ml | 1 fl oz |
| ¼ cup | 60 ml | 2 fl oz |
| ⅓ cup | 80 ml | 2½ fl oz |
| ½ cup | 125 ml | 4 fl oz |
| ⅔ cup | 160 ml | 5 fl oz |
| ¾ cup | 180 ml | 6 fl oz |
| 1 cup | 250 ml | 8 fl oz |
| 2 cups | 500 ml | 16 fl oz |
| 2¼ cups | 560 ml | 20 fl oz |
| 4 cups | 1 litre | 32 fl oz |

### Solids

| Metric | Imperial |
|---|---|
| 15 g | ½ oz |
| 30 g | 1 oz |
| 60 g | 2 oz |
| 125 g | 4 oz |
| 180 g | 6 oz |
| 250 g | 8 oz |
| 500 g | 16 oz (1 lb) |
| 1 kg | 32 oz (2 lb) |

### Millimetres to inches

| Metric | Imperial |
|---|---|
| 3 mm | ⅛ inch |
| 6 mm | ¼ inch |
| 1 cm | ½ inch |
| 2.5 cm | 1 inch |
| 5 cm | 2 inches |
| 18 cm | 7 inches |
| 20 cm | 8 inches |
| 23 cm | 9 inches |
| 25 cm | 10 inches |
| 30 cm | 12 inches |

### Oven temperatures

#### Celsius to Fahrenheit

| Celsius | Fahrenheit |
|---|---|
| 100°C | 200°F |
| 120°C | 250°F |
| 140°C | 275°F |
| 150°C | 300°F |
| 160°C | 325°F |
| 180°C | 350°F |
| 190°C | 375°F |
| 200°C | 400°F |
| 220°C | 425°F |

#### Electric to gas

| Celsius | Gas |
|---|---|
| 110°C | ¼ |
| 130°C | ½ |
| 140°C | 1 |
| 150°C | 2 |
| 170°C | 3 |
| 180°C | 4 |
| 190°C | 5 |
| 200°C | 6 |
| 220°C | 7 |
| 230°C | 8 |
| 240°C | 9 |
| 250°C | 10 |

# Acknowledgements

When I first started cake decorating several years ago I never thought for one minute I would be putting together this book. I would like to thank Laurel Watson who sparked my passion for decorating and believed I could create.

To my two gorgeous boys, Jordon and Bradon, who have had to endure many cupcakes this year — rough, I know! Your unconditional love, support and encouragement in putting this collection together has been invaluable. Jordon, I promise not to wake you in the middle of the night to tell you of another idea. Well, not for a while anyway. Cheers, boys!

I would also like to thank incredibly talented photographer Charlie Smith — through his photography my little cakes have come to life!

And to all of my friends and family who have had to listen to endless hours of cupcake talk. This is just the beginning ...

## *Suppliers*

**Milly's Kitchen Shop**
273 Ponsonby Rd
Ponsonby
Auckland 1011
09 376 1550
www.millyskitchen.co.nz

**Kiwicakes**
1c Grant St
Kamo
Whangarei 0141
09 435 7313
www.kiwicakes.co.nz

**Farro Fresh Food Store**
70 Parkway Drive
Mairangi Bay
Auckland
09 478 0020
www.farrofresh.co.nz

# Index

Baking Tips 10
Ballet Slippers on Quilting Cupcakes 28
Beehive Cupcakes 30
*Buttercream*
  Caramel 130
  Chocolate 135
  How to Pipe 19
  How to Fill a Decorating Bag with 17
  Lemon 135
  Peanut Butter 135
  Vanilla 135
  White 136

*Cake*
  Hokey Pokey 115
  Rich Chocolate 114
  Rich Fruit 117
  Vanilla Bean 116
*Cake Pops*
  Hokey Pokey 104
  How to Make 103
  Ice Cream Sundae 106
  Jaffa 108
  Sheep Pops in a Paddock 110
Caramel Buttercream 130
Carrot Cupcakes 93
Chocolate Buttercream 135
Chocolate Chilli Cupcakes 91
Chocolate Christmas Pudding Cupcakes 32
Chocolate Cupcakes 90
Chocolate Ganache 131
Chocolate Icing 126
Chocolate Jaffa or Spearmint Whoopie Pies 121
Chocolate Kiwi Cupcakes 34
Chocolate Kiwifruit Cupcakes 36
Chocolate Mud Cupcakes 92
Chocolate, How to Melt 19
Colour Icing, How to 14
Coloured Sprinkles, How to Make 17
Conversion Tables 140
Cream Cheese Icing 136
*Cupcakes*
  Ballet Slippers on Quilting 28
  Beehive 30
  Carrot 93

Chocolate 90
Chocolate Chilli 91
Chocolate Christmas Pudding 32
Chocolate Kiwi 34
Chocolate Kiwifruit 36
Chocolate Mud 92
Easter Bunny and Bunnies Down the Hole 39
Fish and Chips 43
Gumboot 46
Hedgehog 48
Honey 94
Huhu Grub 50
Jaffa, Snifter and Pineapple Lump 52
Jandal 54
Kiwi on Blossom with Fern 56
Lemon 95
Marshmallow Sheep 60
Mini Present 62
Peanut Butter 96
Pohutukawa Flowers on Chocolate 66
Pukeko on Leaves 68
Red Velvet 97
Roses on White Buttercream Swirl 72
Rugby Ball and Boots 74
Sand Bucket 76
Sheep in the Shearing Shed 78
Strawberries and Cream 80, 98
Sunflowers 82
Swimming Pool 84
Tomato Sauce Bottle 42
Vanilla 99
Weta 87

Easter Bunny and Bunnies Down the Hole
  Cupcakes 39
Edible Glue, How to Make 17

Fillings for Whoopie Pies 130
Fish and Chips Cupcakes 43
Fondant 12, 134
Fondant, Storing Decorations 12
Fondant, Turning into Modelling Paste 12
Form Basic Shapes, How to 13

Ganache, Chocolate 131

Gumboot Cupcakes 46

Hedgehog Cupcakes 48
Hints and Tips 9
Hokey Pokey 122
Hokey Pokey Cake 115
Hokey Pokey Cake Pops 104
Hokey Pokey Whoopie Pies 122
Honey Cupcakes 94
*How to*
  Colour Icing 14
  Fill a Decorating Bag with Buttercream 17
  Form Basic Shapes 13
  Make Cake Pops 103
  Make Coloured Sprinkles 17
  Make Edible Glue 17
  Melt Chocolate 19
  Pipe Buttercream 19
Huhu Grub Cupcakes 50

Ice Cream Sundae Cake Pops 106
*Icing*
  Chocolate 126
  Cream Cheese 136
  How to Colour 14
  Italian Meringue 138
  Lemon Cream Cheese 136
  Raspberry 126
  Royal 137
  Storing 15
Italian Meringue Icing 138

Jaffa Cake Pops 108
Jaffa, Snifter and Pineapple Lump Cupcakes 52
Jandal Cupcakes 54

Kiwi on Blossom with Fern Cupcakes 56

Lamington Whoopie Pies 124
Lemon Buttercream 135
Lemon Cream Cheese Icing 136
Lemon Cucpakes 95

Marshmallow Sheep Cupcakes 60
Mini Present Cupcakes 62

Modelling Paste, Turning Fondant into 12

Peanut Butter Buttercream 135
Peanut Butter Cupcakes 96
Pohutukawa Flowers on Chocolate Cupcakes 66
Pukeko on Leaves Cupcakes 68

Raspberry Icing 126
Red Velvet Cupcakes 97
Rich Chocolate Cake 114
Rich Fruit Cake 117
Roses on White Buttercream Swirl Cupcakes 72
Royal Icing 137
Rugby Ball and Boots Cupcakes 74

Sand Bucket Cupcakes 76
Sheep in the Shearing Shed Cupcakes 78
Sheep Pops in a Paddock 110
Storing Fondant Decorations 12
Storing Icing 15
Strawberries and Cream Cupcakes 80, 98
Sugar Syrup 138
Sunflowers Cupcakes 82
Swimming Pool Cupcakes 84
Syrup, Sugar 138

Tomato Sauce Bottle Cupcakes 42
Tools and Equipment 20

Vanilla Bean Cake 116
Vanilla Buttercream 135
Vanilla Cupcakes 99
Vanilla Whoopie Pies 128

Weta Cupcakes 87
What is a Whoopie Pie 118
White Buttercream 136
Whoopie Pie, What is a 118
*Whoopie Pies*
  Chocolate Jaffa or Spearmint 121
  Hokey Pokey 122
  Lamington 124
  Vanilla 128

Kirsten Day has a passion for food which began as a child. She can still remember winning an award for her sponge at the local show day.

Kirsten studied catering at Waikato Polytechnic before travelling widely overseas, attending Wilton training classes in Asia and Australia, and exploring cake decorating techniques with Squires Kitchen International School and Knightsbridge PME in England. She has attended several classes with accomplished decorators Debbie Brown and Patti Clark.

Kirsten is a qualified Wilton Method cake decorating tutor and is in the Wilton Hall of Fame. She teaches cake decorating and cooking skills at Milly's Kitchen Shop in Auckland and around the country.

She lives on the North Shore with her two teenage boys.